THE DEADLY GAME

BY JAMES YAFFE

ADAPTED FROM THE NOVEL *TRAPPS*
BY FRIEDRICH DÜRRENMATT

★

★

DRAMATISTS
PLAY SERVICE
INC.

THE DEADLY GAME was first presented by Alton Wilkes and Joe Manchester in association with Emil Coleman at the Longacre Theatre, New York City, on February 2, 1960. It was directed by William Gaskill. The production was designed and lighted by Wolfgang Roth. The cast was as follows:

EMILE CARPEAU	Ludwig Donath
BERNARD LAROQUE	Claude Dauphin
JOSEPH PILLET	Pat Malone
PIERRE	Frank Campanella
HOWARD TRAPP	Pat Hingle
GUSTAVE KUMMER	Max Adrian
A VISITOR	Frances Helm

A slightly revised version of THE DEADLY GAME was first presented by Alton Wilkes and Jim Mendenhall Productions at the Provincetown Playhouse, in New York City, on February 13, 1966. It was directed by Mr. Wilkes; sets and lighting were by Richard Jackson; and the Executive Technical Director was Ben Wampler. The cast, in order of appearance, was as follows:

EMILE CARPEAU	Albert M. Ottenheimer
BERNARD LAROQUE	Rudolf Weiss
JOSEPH PILLET	Lance Cunard
NICOLE	Jana Klenburg
HOWARD TRAPP	Chet London
GUSTAVE KUMMER	Roger De Koven
PIERRE	Michael O'Dowd
A VISITOR	Paula Shaw

The text of the play, in the present edition, is that which was used in the above production.
The action takes place in the house of Emile Carpeau in the Swiss Alps.

ACT I
A winter evening.

ACT II
SCENE 1: The same evening.
SCENE 2: Several days later.

CHARACTERS

HOWARD TRAPP: In his thirties or early forties, good-looking, with a genial self-assured manner, a kind of charm which comes from his vitality and apparent confidence.

THE JUDGE: In his late sixties, a benign cheerful old man. His manner is amiable, almost cherubic at moments, but as we get to know him we sense more and more his dignity, his self-possession, his inner strength, the strength of one who is able to make important decisions and arbitrate vital questions.

THE DEFENSE ATTORNEY: In his late sixties, a small man who seems quiet and unassuming at first glance but turns out to have a deeply emotional nature. His moods vary sharply from melancholy despair to immense boyish enthusiasm.

THE PROSECUTOR: In his late sixties, tall, stiffly formal in manner, with a constant sense of deep emotions always rigidly under control. In his rigid politeness, his razor-sharp logic, his cold adherence to law and to duty, his relentless exploitation of every advantage when he is prosecuting a case, the compelling force of his eloquence, he seems almost inhuman.

THE OLD MAN: In his seventies, mild, gentle, just slightly senile.

PIERRE: In his forties, a mute; ungainly, strong, friendly, but with a suggestion of violence underneath.

A VISITOR: In her thirties, smartly dressed, perfectly poised, cold as ice.

NICOLE: In her late twenties, attractive, French accent, provocative and flirtatious, but not blatantly.

THE DEADLY GAME

ACT I

The curtain goes up on a dark stage. In the darkness the clock is heard striking solemnly seven times. As it strikes, the LIGHTS *go up slowly, revealing the Judge's living room. The atmosphere is vaguely sinister at first, but with more light it soon becomes bright, cozy, homelike. The suggestion of a snowstorm raging outside is visible through the windows.*

A festive-looking dinner table is set up in the alcove. In an armchair, L., *the Old Man, in his evening clothes, is dozing gently, his head down.*

At a table in the R. *of the room, the Judge and the Defense Attorney sit across a chessboard. The Attorney is studying the board intently, while the Judge leans back, relaxed and smiling. At last the Attorney reaches out to move a piece. The Judge stops him by shaking his head disapprovingly and uttering "uh uh." The Attorney pulls back his hand, studies the board a moment longer, then moves a different piece. The Judge, without a moment's thought, moves a piece of his own. The Attorney sighs and starts pondering again.*

Nicole comes in from the kitchen L., *holding two dusty bottles of wine. The Judge sees her, beams. The Attorney continues to study the chessboard.*

JUDGE. (*Stepping towards Nicole* L.) Ah, thank you, Nicole. Now let's see, which shall it be, the Chambertin or Medoc—which goes better with roast goose? The Chambertin, I think. I'm in a festive mood tonight. Now let's see if the table is properly set. (*He bustles over to the table and starts checking the silverware, nap-*

kins, etc.) Forks, spoons— Napkins! Good Heavens, Nicole, we completely forgot the napkins!

NICOLE. "I'm sorry, Monsieur, I thought Pierre put them on the table." (*Nicole gets napkins. Meanwhile, the Attorney has made another move.*)

ATTORNEY. All ready, Emile.

JUDGE. At your service. (*He goes over to the chessboard and makes his move. The Attorney starts to ponder deeply again. Just then the Old Man, in his corner, breaks sharply out of his doze.*)

OLD MAN. (*Blinks in confusion, then realizes where he is.*) I dozed off, didn't I? (*Looks around, a puzzled note in his voice.*) Where's Gustave? I don't see Gustave.

JUDGE. (*Approaching the Old Man,* L.) He hasn't arrived yet, Joseph. (*Nicole enters with napkins.*)

ATTORNEY. (*Looking up gloomily from the chessboard.*) Furthermore he isn't going to arrive.

OLD MAN. (*Quite alarmed.*) But he *has* to arrive! We can do nothing without him!

JUDGE. (*Reassuringly.*) He is certain to be here. He is simply delayed by the storm. Nicole, put the oil lamp outside the door just to be sure and tell Pierre to check this window, it's been rattling a bit. . . . (*Returning to chess table,* C.) Really, Bernard, you mustn't upset Joseph with your congenital pessimism.

ATTORNEY. (*Sheepishly.*) I am sorry, Emile. I *am* allowing my pessimism to get the best of me. It's because I look forward to these evenings so much.

JUDGE. Well, that is nothing to be ashamed of. I feel the same way. I spent the last two days planning the dinner.

ATTORNEY. But you have control over your emotions. That is the great curse of my life. If I feel sad, I drown everyone around me in tears. If I feel happy, I have difficulty restraining myself from dancing a jig. (*Sighs, turns back to the chessboard.*) Well, I can think of nothing better than this. (*Makes a move.*)

JUDGE. (*Instantly countering with another move.*) And what do you say to *this?*

NICOLE. (*Enters with lantern.*) Pierre will fasten the window, Monsieur.

JUDGE. Thank you, Nicole. (*She goes out front door with lantern, hangs it up, and returns to kitchen. The Attorney shakes his *head in despair and once again becomes absorbed in studying the board.)*

OLD MAN. (*Shivering.*) It's cold. It's really very cold. (*Judge covers Joseph with blanket.*) I can't remember when it was so cold before. Not since the winter of 1911— (*Attorney makes a move on the chessboard.*)

ATTORNEY. Well, I've done it. My last desperate attempt. (*The doorbell rings. The three men look up instantly, with expressions of excitement and relief. Nicole starts out of the room. Attorney, with a smile.*) Well, he's here. Thank Heaven!

OLD MAN. Yes—thank Heaven!

JUDGE. (*Starts up the steps.*) I'll welcome him. Meanwhile, (*At top step.*) Bernard, prepare to begin your jig. (*Judge opens door. Howard Trapp is there. He is covered with snow, breathing hard, red with cold.*)

TRAPP. Excuse me—can you help me? (*Enters.*) I was wondering—

JUDGE. Good Heavens, what's the trouble here?

TRAPP. Sorry to barge in on you. My car hit a snow drift. If you could put me up till the storm's over—

JUDGE. Of course we can, my dear sir. Nicole, help the gentleman with his coat.

TRAPP. (*As she helps him.*) Thanks . . . (*Entering foyer.*) I was driving down to Geneva. I smashed up about a half mile down the road. (*He takes off galoshes.*)

JUDGE. It is a miracle that you saw our lights. This road is most treacherous. The house is built on the edge of a precipice.

TRAPP. I am lucky at that. My God. I could be at the bottom of an Alp by now.

JUDGE. Fortunately that is all behind you. No cold inhospitable Alp for you tonight, my dear sir. (*Joseph wraps blanket around himself and rises to front of fire.*)

TRAPP. My name is Trapp. Howard Trapp. That's with two P's.

JUDGE. Delighted to meet you, Mr. Trapp. I am Emile Carpeau—only one P, I fear. I welcome you to my home.

TRAPP. This is really very nice of you, Mr. Carpeau.

JUDGE. Won't you step into the living room and take advantage of the fire. (*Steps in 1 step ahead of Trapp.*) Gentlemen—we have an unexpected but welcome guest. This is Mr. Howard Trapp. Mr.

Trapp, may I present my old friends, who occasionally share these winter evenings with me. Mr. Bernard Laroque—

TRAPP. (*Shaking the Attorney's hand.*) How are you? (*Nicole exits.*)

ATTORNEY. Very well, thank you, Mr. Trapp. We certainly never expected to have a visitor on a night like *this.*

JUDGE. And this is the elder statesman of our little group—my respected friend Joseph Pillet. In our hearts we all have a special place for Joseph.

TRAPP. (*Holding out his hand.*) Glad to meet you—

OLD MAN. (*Not taking his hand, but staring at him intently. Crosses in front of Judge to Trapp.*) Are you a friend of Gustave? Did Gustave bring you with him?

JUDGE. Gustave is still not here. Mr. Trapp is a motorist who was unfortunately caught in the storm.

OLD MAN. (*With quickened excitement turns to Judge.*) A stranger? He's a stranger?

JUDGE. Yes, he is.

OLD MAN. And he's going to join us tonight? (*To Trapp.*) I am so happy, Monsieur. We have been waiting such a long time.

TRAPP. (*Puzzled.*) Waiting—?

JUDGE. (*Stepping in smoothly turns and leads Joseph to* U.C. *chair.*) Joseph means that we see so few strangers here, we wait anxiously for each new face. Won't you move closer to the fire, Mr. Trapp?

TRAPP. Thanks. (*Trapp goes to the fire* L., *and warms himself. This gives the Judge and the Attorney an opportunity to exchange a significant look. The Attorney starts to say something, but the Judge motions him to silence and turns to Trapp at* C.)

JUDGE. Well, my good sir, you're a great distance from your native New York, aren't you?

TRAPP. Say, that's pretty good! Most people over here can't tell one American from another!

JUDGE. (*Amused.*) I have traveled extensively, and I have learned to recognize the various regional types.

ATTORNEY. I spent some time in your city when I was a much younger man, Mr. Trapp. I studied for one year at your famous Columbia University.

TRAPP. Oh, yes.

ATTORNEY. I enjoyed some happy experiences there. (*Quite solemnly.*) It was there that I learned about women.

TRAPP. (*Amused.*) You don't say so.

ATTORNEY. It's quite true. Switzerland is no place to learn about women—every young man should go to America for that purpose.

TRAPP. Your Swiss women seem to be most attractive . . . that little maid of yours, for instance.

JUDGE. Oh, Nicole? Yes, she is an attractive girl. Somewhat too interested in clothes and dancing perhaps . . . (*He breaks off as Nicole reenters with tray of sherry glasses and salt and pepper shakers for table.*) From your appearance, Mr. Trapp, I suspect that a little cognac would suit you nicely.

TRAPP. You won't get any argument from me. (*The Judge signals Nicole, who crosses to bar, puts down sherry glasses, picks up prepoured brandy snifter, and brings it to Trapp. She then exits.*)

JUDGE. Ordinarily we don't drink our first glass until all of us have arrived—but this is a special occasion—

TRAPP. You're expecting someone else?

ATTORNEY. Oh yes, Mr. Trapp. *If* he gets here! He's half an hour late already!

JUDGE. He'll get here, Bernard.

ATTORNEY. But soon the snow will be too thick—

TRAPP. Say, this is sort of embarrassing. (*Crosses* U. C.) I can just as easily pass the time in another room, you know.

JUDGE. But why on earth, Mr. Trapp?

TRAPP. (*Backs a little* U. L.) Well, I seem to be breaking in on your party—

JUDGE. Nonsense.

ATTORNEY. Parties are so much more enjoyable when they give us a chance to meet new people. (*Joseph rises.*)

OLD MAN. (*Almost pleadingly crossing to Trapp.*) Please, Mr. Trapp, you must stay with us.

TRAPP. (*Rather flattered.*) Well, sure—if you really want me to. (*He laughs, and they all join in amiably. Then Trapp drinks, rubs his hands together.*) I can see why you look forward to strangers up here. This place is really out in the middle of nowhere, isn't it?

JUDGE. (*Crosses* D. L.) That is precisely what I like best about it, Mr. Trapp. (*Joseph crosses behind to Trapp's* R.)

TRAPP. Wouldn't satisfy me. (*Crosses* U. C.) I like people, action, places to go.

JUDGE. Only natural, at your age. When I was a young man, how I loved to surround myself with people! But the years have made me—more selective. (*Joseph sits* U. R.)
ATTORNEY. I have never been able to achieve a balanced attitude toward people. Almost seventy years of disillusionment have failed to destroy one bit of my delight in the human race.
TRAPP. With me there's never been any disillusionment. I never had any illusions in the first place.
JUDGE. I do hope you're not a cynic. So many in your type of work are inclined to be cynical.
TRAPP. I'm sorry, but I don't believe I said anything about my type of work.
JUDGE. Why, you're a salesman, aren't you?
TRAPP. I'll be damned! (*Crosses* D. C.)
JUDGE. What is the popular American expression? A "traveling salesman"?
TRAPP. How did you know that?
JUDGE. My apologies, Mr. Trapp. I've trained myself to notice things. (*Encircling Trapp to Trapp's* R. *Trapp counters.*) The cut of your clothes, your manner of speaking, of holding yourself—all these things cry out to me, "salesman."
ATTORNEY. I fear you've stumbled on a nest of trained observers, Mr. Trapp. We are all retired lawyers, you see, and a legal career obliges one to be a student of human nature.
TRAPP. I'm a student of human nature myself. In my business you have to be. You'll never make any sales unless you're able to size a man up and find out his weaknesses. (*Laughs, rather pleased with himself.*) I never had much to do with the law, though. I was brought up in a neighborhood where everybody ran when they saw the law coming. (*He laughs, and the others join in.*)
JUDGE. Yes, this attitude is most common—even among the law-abiding Swiss.
ATTORNEY. (*Rises, crosses to* D. C.) If only people would realize that the law can be their friend, their best hope in time of trouble. It need not be cold and heartless—
JUDGE. Bernard, Bernard—Mr. Trapp is tired and wet—I doubt if he is in the mood for philosophical discussion. (*Crosses* U. L. *to door.*)
ATTORNEY. Yes, of course. Forgive me, Mr. Trapp. I get carried away sometimes. (*Crosses* D. R. *to table.*)

JUDGE. (*Calls off* L.) Nicole . . . If you have finished your cognac, Mr. Trapp, (*Nicole enters.*) Nicole will show you to your room—undoubtedly you'll want to refresh yourself before dinner. The large bedroom at the top of the stairs, Nicole. (*She goes up, followed by Trapp. He is stopped at top step by . . .*) I hope the dinner will please you, Mr. Trapp. When my friends come to visit me, I like to preside over the cuisine and make little experiments.

ATTORNEY. Emile's little experiments are the supreme moments of our existence.

JUDGE. You flatter me, Bernard—but I am no hypocrite, so I cannot deny that I deserve it.

OLD MAN. (*Alarmed.*) He's not going, is he? You haven't asked him yet—

JUDGE. (*Gently.*) Later, later, Joseph. (*To Trapp.*) Won't you follow Nicole, Mr. Trapp. (*Trapp starts up, is stopped short by . . .*) And there is hot water.

TRAPP. I'm sure glad to hear *that*. Incidentally—do you happen to have a phone in the house? I ought to call my wife and tell her what's happened.

JUDGE. You were on your way to join your wife?

TRAPP. No—she's staying at the ski resort, on top of the mountain. (*Gestures off* L.) I was driving down to Geneva for a business appointment.

JUDGE. I'm so sorry, Mr. Trapp, but I've never felt the need for a telephone.

TRAPP. Well, it isn't important. (*Starts out then turns back.*) I don't know how I can ever pay you back for your hospitality.

JUDGE. (*With a smile.*) Who knows, Mr. Trapp? We may think of something. (*Trapp follows Nicole upstairs* R. *The 3 men exchange glances.*)

OLD MAN. (*Going to the Judge.*) Emile, don't you think—? (*The Judge motions the Old Man to silence. Waits till Trapp is out of hearing, goes up a step or two, turns back to them:*)

JUDGE. Well, my gloomy friends, so much for your pessimism, eh?

ATTORNEY. May I remind you that Gustave still isn't here. (*Crosses* D. R.)

OLD MAN. (*Almost in panic. To Attorney.*) But he *will* come! It would be too terrible if he didn't come *now!*

JUDGE. (*Crosses to them at table.*) Quite right, Joseph. Fate couldn't possibly be so cruel as to deprive us of Gustave now that we have Mr. Trapp.

OLD MAN. (*His optimism reviving.*) He's possible, isn't he, Emile? What do you think?

JUDGE. He seems to have possibilities.

OLD MAN. What do *you* think, Bernard? He is possible, isn't he?

ATTORNEY. No, I don't think he is, Joseph. (*Sits at chess table.*)

JUDGE. Now why are you so positive of that? (*Crosses* D. C.)

ATTORNEY. Because the moment I set eyes on Mr. Trapp I liked him. If he were truly possible I couldn't have liked him, could I?

JUDGE. You like everybody the moment you set eyes on them. Do you remember last year? That philosophy professor from the Sorbonne?

ATTORNEY. (*Sheepishly.*) Well, yes, I confess that I did go a bit overboard in that instance. He was such a cultured, softspoken gentleman.

JUDGE. I don't criticize you, Bernard. How could we accomplish anything if it weren't for your indestructible faith in people? I merely say that Mr. Trapp may turn out to be more of a possibility than you anticipate. (*Joseph crosses to* U. C. *chair.*)

ATTORNEY. (*Beginning to be on the defensive.*) But what have you got against him?

JUDGE. You observed his clothes, no doubt. Very expensive material. Our new friend would seem to be a most successful man. (*Joseph sits.*)

ATTORNEY. (*Reacting instantly. Crosses* U. C. *to Judge.*) Success is not necessarily incriminating. We established that precedent a long time ago.

JUDGE. Of course we did—I remember how hard you fought for it in the case of that Italian banker. I simply find Mr. Trapp's success to be a suggestive circumstance, a vague indication—

ATTORNEY. (*Crosses back to chess table.*) I have no trust in suggestive circumstances and vague indications. Human beings are entitled to better than that— (*He is interrupted by the doorbell. Judge starts to the front door* R.)

OLD MAN. Is that him? Is that Gustave? (*Judge starts up steps.*)

JUDGE. I shouldn't be a bit surprised. (*Almost mischievously. At top step.*) Now we won't tell him about Mr. Trapp. We'll see how long it takes him to guess what's happened.

OLD MAN. (*Crosses* D. L. *to chair.*) Gustave will know it right away. Gustave knows *everything.* (*Nicole opens the front door* R., *as the Judge reaches the foyer. The Prosecutor comes in, cold, wet. Nicole helps him with his coat.*)

PROSECUTOR. Excuse my tardiness, Emile. I had some difficulty with a snowdrift.

JUDGE. Quite all right, Gustave. (*He walks down steps.*) We're delighted to see you.

NICOLE. Permit me to help you, Monsieur Gustave.

PROSECUTOR. Thank you, Nichole . . . It's a nightmare outside. I nearly fell three times. (*Removes boots.*) I certainly won't be stirring out of this house tonight. (*Starts down steps into room, Nicole follows him, picking up Trapp's empty glass.*) Ah, everyone safe and sound, I see. You're positively blooming tonight, Nicole. I've never seen you look so lovely.

NICOLE. Thank you, Monsieur.

JUDGE. Nicole tells me that her headaches are all gone.

PROSECUTOR. Of course they are. Now instead of headaches, she has us.

NICOLE. (*Embarrassed.*) If you will excuse me . . . (*She exits with glass.*)

PROSECUTOR. She's improving, isn't she? It's most gratifying . . . You look particularly well tonight, Joseph. This weather appears to agree with you.

ATTORNEY. The important thing is, does this weather agree with *you,* Gustave? We want you to be at your best tonight.

PROSECUTOR. I will be, have no fear. As soon as I satisfy my ravenous hunger. (*Starts sniffing the air.*) Do I smell my favorite? Asparagus a la Carpeau? Yes—it's near—it's very near— (*He starts moving toward the kitchen* L., *as if pulled by an invisible force.*)

JUDGE. (*Laughing, intercepting him.*) No, no, Gustave, not just yet. Tonight you must earn your supper. No food until you give a little demonstration of your talent for finding out secrets.

PROSECUTOR. Ah—my big nose, you mean.

ATTORNEY. We have a secret for you tonight, Gustave.

OLD MAN. Bernard thinks you won't guess it. (*Sits.*)

PROSECUTOR. (*Smiling.*) Won't I, my dear Bernard? (*Attention on chessboard.*) Very well, my friends—where is he?

ATTORNEY. (*In a weak voice.*) Who?

PROSECUTOR. The stranger who arrived just before me—the American gentleman. Black's move? (*He moves a piece.*) Checkmate, I think.

JUDGE. Bravo!

ATTORNEY. It's black magic. You must have a crystal ball.

PROSECUTOR. Not a crystal ball. (*Crosses* U. R.) Merely a casual glance at the unfamiliar overcoat of decidedly (*Crosses back* C.) American cut which even now is dripping water in the hall.

ATTORNEY. Oh well, you were lucky.

JUDGE. (*Crossing to bar.*) No, no, we must give the devil his due. Gustave, you well deserve a glass of sherry. (*He pours sherry and hands it around, as the conversation continues.*)

OLD MAN. Bernard and Emile disagree about him, Gustave. Bernard thinks he isn't possible, but Emile isn't so sure.

PROSECUTOR. And what do *you* think, Joseph?

OLD MAN. Well—I think he is possible. He's a traveling salesman, and he has a great deal of money, and he doesn't seem to like lawyers very much, and he drinks cognac as if it were water— (*Offstage* R. *slam. Trapp is heard coming down the stairs* R. *The Judge gestures for silence.*)

JUDGE. Hush, Joseph, he's coming. Gustave, observe him awhile. We're depending on your opinion.

PROSECUTOR. (*With a nod of acknowledgement. Crosses* U. *to above* L. *chair.*) It will be a pleasure. (*Trapp enters to top step, cleaned up, wearing a newly-pressed pair of pants. The Judge bustles up to him.*)

JUDGE. Well, you are somewhat refreshed, my dear sir?

TRAPP. I certainly feel a lot better. Oh, by the way, the bottoms of my pants were soaking wet, and I saw this suit hanging in the closet, so I just borrowed the pants.

JUDGE. Quite all right. (*Trapp comes down.*) The suit was left here by a guest awhile ago. Mr. Trapp, I'd like you to meet the fourth member of our little group—my dear friend, Mr. Gustave Kummer.

PROSECUTOR. (*Bowing to Trapp.*) Charmed.

TRAPP. How are you? I've been hearing a lot about you.

PROSECUTOR. And I about you, Mr. Trapp. I understand that you're not particularly fond of lawyers.
TRAPP. Oh, I've got nothing against them, sometimes I wish I'd gone in for it myself. (*Jokingly.*) Whenever big money changes hands, there's always some lawyer involved.
PROSECUTOR. So I have been told. But that is an aspect of the profession with which none of us, I'm afraid, was ever familiar. (*All chuckle. Judge crosses to bar, brings back a glass for Trapp and himself.*) Our field is—or I should say was—criminal law.
TRAPP. Just like in the movies, huh? "Where were you on the night of the murder?" (*Takes glass offered by Judge.*) Thank you.
JUDGE. (*Smiling.*) Well, not always quite so melodramatic.
PROSECUTOR. (*Somewhat sternly. Crossing* D. L.) Law is the exercise of justice according to logic and precedent. Melodrama plays no part in it whatsoever.
ATTORNEY. (*Argumentatively.*) But that's not true. A courtroom isn't a chessboard. It's filled with people, not with wooden pieces. Tears and laughter, hatred and love, everything you call melodrama, in fact—they're all part of life, and they will find their way into a courtroom no matter what you do to shut them out.
PROSECUTOR. (*Dryly.*) Mice will find their way into an old house too—but is that a valid argument against keeping a cat? (*Attorney puts chess pieces into box.*)
JUDGE. Gentlemen, gentlemen. (*Crosses to* L. *of Trapp.*) I'm afraid you'll just have to get used to these little conflicts. Gustave and Bernard have been flying at each other's throats for thirty years. For a long time they were paid to do so.
TRAPP. How's that?
JUDGE. Until my retirement, I was Judge of the Criminal Court of the municipality of Geneva. Gustave was our Chief Prosecutor —a terror to the criminal elements for miles around—and Bernard (*Crosses to Attorney.*) was our Public Defender, for many years the most famous criminal lawyer in Switzerland.
ATTORNEY. You must not listen to Emile. Friendship leads him to exaggerate.
JUDGE. Bernard carries modesty to the point of obsession. Converse with him in a drawing room, and you would unhesitatingly assume him to be as meek as a lamb.
PROSECUTOR. (*Wryly.*) A dangerous assumption, believe me. There are those of us who remember to our regret how the lamb

rose to address a crowded courtroom, and suddenly his voice became the roar of a lion.

ATTORNEY. (*Crosses* L. *to him at back of* L. *chair.*) Yes, but what of all the times you pulled the lion by the tail and turned him back into a lamb again? (*Pats him on back.*)

JUDGE. Gentlemen, we're talking too much about ourselves. We're forgetting how important it is to show an interest in our guest. (*Pulls out* L. *chair at chess table for Trapp.*) Wouldn't it be *possible* to talk to Mr. Trapp about something more interesting, Gustave?

PROSECUTOR. (*Acknowledging the hint with a knowing nod.*) Of course, I forgot myself. (*Puts down glass on table and crosses* C. *to Trapp.*) Your own profession interests me enormously, Mr. Trapp. I envy you your opportunities to travel, see new places, meet all kinds of people.

TRAPP. I've been around all right. But as far as I can see, people are about the same wherever you go.

PROSECUTOR. You feel that we all have a certain common humanity which is more important than our individual differences?

TRAPP. Well, actually I was thinking in terms of sales technique. When you're trying to sell a piece of merchandise, it doesn't matter if the customer is rich or poor, young or old, there are three things you always have to make him believe. One: that he's getting this product for a lot less than it's worth. Two: that all the people he looks up to in the world have got one. And, three: that his best friends are going to cut him dead if he doesn't have one.

PROSECUTOR. (*Crossing to above chess table.*) In short, greed, envy, and fear—these, in your opinion, are the mainsprings of human conduct?

TRAPP. That's not an opinion. That's experience.

ATTORNEY. But surely you can't mean that, Mr. Trapp. What of the higher, nobler feelings of mankind? You can't discount all of *them.*

TRAPP. *I'm* not discounting them. *I'm* in favor of them. It's the people I meet who discount them.

PROSECUTOR. A plain blunt philosophy. (*Crossing back to* C.) You're emphatically a product of the Twentieth Century, aren't you? (*He turns to the others, speaking significantly.*) It's really quite fortunate for us that Mr. Trapp's car broke down tonight. I have an idea that we're going to have a most stimulating evening.

ATTORNEY. You really think so, Gustave?

PROSECUTOR. I have seldom been so sure of anything in my life!

OLD MAN. (*Rising between the two men.*) Then he's possible. I knew he was going to be possible.

JUDGE. Joseph—

TRAPP. Possible? I don't follow.

JUDGE. Joseph has an old-fashioned frankness that sometimes disconcerts people. When he finds it *possible* to be friendly with a man he comes right out and says so.

OLD MAN. (*Crossing to* U. R. *chair in back of Judge.*) I had a feeling in my bones when I woke up this morning. I knew that the day would turn out well. (*Nicole appears in the kitchen doorway* L. *The Judge crosses to her.*)

JUDGE. Ah, Nicole—all ready for us.

NICOLE. Yes, Monsieur.

JUDGE. Then you may begin. (*To Trapp, as Nicole returns to kitchen.*) You are fond of roast goose, I hope?

TRAPP. The way I feel right now, I could eat *live* goose.

JUDGE. (*Crossing* R *to bar.*) No such feat will be required of you. I have made a special sauce—my *sauce printemps a la Carpeau.* The secret is in the oregano. (*Nicole carries in the buffet dinner.*)

TRAPP. (*Jumping* U. C. *to help.*) Let me help you with that.

NICOLE. Thank you, it isn't necessary, Monsieur.

JUDGE. But before we begin, I think we must all have a glass of wine—

OLD MAN. (*Impatiently.*) Aren't we going to eat? The sooner we eat, the sooner we can—

JUDGE. Right away, Joseph. In his old age, Joseph has reverted to the appetite (*Nicole crosses to bar, gets tray of 3 prepoured wine glasses, crosses with them to Prosecutor, Attorney, then Trapp.*) of his childhood. I feel sure you'll like this. It's a rare vintage. This is almost the last of the stock I inherited from my father.

ATTORNEY. (*To the wine glass.*) Everything is fading away. All the good old things.

PROSECUTOR. (*With a sense of underlying significance. Catching Trapp and Nicole flirting out of the corner of his eye.*) And all the good old moral values—which is far more important.

ATTORNEY. (*With a twinkle.*) Yes, Gustave, no doubt you are right. Yet I confess it, sometimes I feel that I would gladly spare the moral values if only I could halt the disappearance of the wine.

JUDGE. (*Raises his glass.*) Gentlemen—a small toast in Mr. Trapp's honor. To our distinguished guest—and the wonderful stroke of fortune that brought him to us tonight. (*They all lift their glasses, but only Trapp drinks. He notices this, eyes them looking at him, then the rest drink.*) Come, gentlemen, shall we commence to serve ourselves. (*Joseph sits. The rest move up to the buffet table* U. C. *As the talk goes on, they serve themselves, with Nicole helping them.*)

TRAPP. You really treat yourselves well up here.

JUDGE. I try my best, Mr. Trapp. I can heartily recommend the croustade de champignons. (*Judge hands Joseph's plate to Nicole.*) You know, Mr. Trapp, we weren't always such heavy eaters. A few years ago our appetites were quite feeble—before we started playing our game. (*Crosses to behind chess table.*)

TRAPP. What sort of game do you play? Charades or cards or something like that?

OLD MAN. Oh, no! Our game is much more exciting! You'll find out when—

JUDGE. When you hear all the details. Of course, ours is a rather unusual game. (*Trapp sits.*) It may be that you will find it a little —absurd.

TRAPP. I've played some pretty silly games in my day—you know, late at night, when everybody's got a few too many drinks in them! (*He laughs and the others join in. Nicole gives Judge his plate.*)

PROSECUTOR. (*Watching Trapp intently.*) I knew it the moment I set eyes on you, Mr. Trapp. You are a man who likes to drink deep of experience.

TRAPP. I'm a man who likes to have a good time if that's what you mean. You only live once is what *I* say. So go on, tell me more about your game.

JUDGE. It consists briefly of this: We gather together in the evenings and play at our former jobs—at law court.

TRAPP. (*Smiling with condescension.*) Sort of like kids playing cops and robbers—meaning no offense.

JUDGE. No offense taken. There *is* a certain element of childishness in our game. Yet there is also a certain fascination (*All nod.*)—as I think you will agree.

TRAPP. But what do you *do,* exactly?

JUDGE. We re-enact the famous trials of history—the trial of Socrates, the trial of Joan of Arc, the Dreyfus Affair—Gustave presents the evidence for the prosecution, Bernard presents the evidence for the defense, and as Judge of the Court I arrive at a verdict and deliver the appropriate sentence.

ATTORNEY. (*Enthusiastically.*) The game gets quite exciting sometimes. We shout and argue back and forth, just as if we were in a real courtroom.

PROSECUTOR. (*Rising.*) And we frequently come to conclusions which disagree with those of the original trial.

ATTORNEY. Only last month Gustave proved conclusively that Julius Caesar wasn't assassinated by his political enemies. It was his wife who managed it—out of jealousy over that Cleopatra affair.

PROSECUTOR. (*Offhandedly modest. To Attorney.*) A clearcut demonstration of a psychological principle which has always proved useful to me—never trust a woman who claims to be above suspicion.

ATTORNEY. Two months ago we tried Hitler—very exciting. Although, I must confess, I could never quite warm up to my client.

JUDGE. The month before it was Judas Iscariot.

ATTORNEY. I got him off.

PROSECUTOR. On a technicality.

ATTORNEY. Tonight we were planning to try Marie Antoinette. I have already prepared a heart-rending opening address . . .

OLD MAN. Three or four evenings a week we play our game.

TRAPP. Three or four evenings? (*Rises, crosses* U. C. *and puts empty dish on buffet table.*) Don't your wives object?

JUDGE. Alas, we face no such obstacle. We are all widowers, living alone in big houses on the mountain—except Gustave, who is a bachelor.

ATTORNEY. That's why Gustave has such a strong belief in a logical universe—he has never lived for any length of time with a woman.

PROSECUTOR. But seriously, Mr. Trapp, our game is far more than mere entertainment. Our lives depend on it. (*Puts empty plate on* D. L. *table.*)

TRAPP. Your lives? That's pretty extreme!

ATTORNEY. (*Rises and puts plate down on Prosecutor's.*) Gustave doesn't exaggerate. Five years ago, we were forced to retire because of our age. In retirement we soon became physical wrecks. Gustave and I were obliged to watch our blood pressure, the doctors suspected our good friend Emile of having diabetes, and poor Joseph was a martyr to his arthritis.

PROSECUTOR. With nothing to do, no purpose in life, our souls as well as our bodies began to atrophy. Physically and spiritually, idleness was killing us.

JUDGE. In short, a sad collection of old fossils. (*Puts down plate on chess table.*) And then we got the idea of playing this game. It was Gustave's idea.

PROSECUTOR. (*Crossing* R. *to between Judge* [R.] *and Trapp* [R. C.].) No, no, you give me too much credit. The idea sprang into all our minds at once—as if by a miracle.

ATTORNEY. (*Growing more excited. Crossing* C. *to Trapp.*) A strange illogical word to hear from *you,* Gustave—but it *was* a miracle! (*Takes Trapp by the arm and leads him* D. R.) Would you believe it, Mr. Trapp, our little game turned out to be the fountain of youth. Within a few short months our stomachs, our livers, our pancreases put themselves in order. Boredom disappeared, appetite returned, and I venture to say that today we're the youngest men of our age in all Europe.

PROSECUTOR. (*Crossing* D. *to them.*) Younger, in a sense, than we were in our prime. After grinding away for years in the courts of the outside world, we are finally able to practice law in its purest form.

JUDGE. (*With a smile. Crossing to bar and pouring Trapp another glass of wine.*) Mr. Trapp, you need some more wine. Good wine is one of life's chief joys, but I think that few people in your country have yet acquired the habit. (*Handing glass to Trapp.*)

TRAPP. (*Holding glass out for still more wine in it.*) Pour away, Judge. One thing I've never had trouble with—acquiring bad habits.

PROSECUTOR. (*Watching Trapp closely as the Judge pours the wine* R.) I believe it.

OLD MAN. The game, the game!

JUDGE. Yes, of course. We're most anxious to hear your reaction, Mr. Trapp. (*The old men lean forward eagerly. Trapp is flattered by their interest.*)

TRAPP. Well, it sounds pretty lively at that. An intellectual sort of game—it might be fun.

JUDGE. Do you really think so? You aren't just being polite?

TRAPP. Absolutely not.

JUDGE. We were hoping you'd feel that way! Now (*Pause.*) why don't you play along with us?

TRAPP. And spoil your fun? No, no, I'd just as soon watch *you* play— (*Sits down on chair* L. *of chess table.*)

PROSECUTOR. (*Moving in to Trapp a step.*) I doubt that, Mr. Trapp. If I read your character correctly, you're not the spectator type. You won't be content unless you're a player, right in the middle of the fray.

TRAPP. I'm not afraid of competition, if that's what you mean. But I'm not a lawyer. I don't have any legal experience or anything.

OLD MAN. But you must play!—the whole evening would be ruined without you!

JUDGE. (*Resuming seat.*) That's right, Mr. Trapp. You see—challenging as it is to recreate the famous trials of history, it is an even greater challenge when we have live material to work with.

TRAPP. Live material?

ATTORNEY. (*Crosses to* U. R. C. *by Trapp's shoulder.*) Exactly. That is when our most interesting situations arise—when a real person stands before our court. (*Crosses a step to behind chair.*)

PROSECUTOR. (*Crosses in a step. Trapp is surrounded now.*) One may practice continually on the rifle range, so to speak—but the true thrill comes only when one pits oneself against a quarry who can shoot back.

TRAPP. You mean you've actually played this game with real people—?

JUDGE. We most certainly have. The last time—to give you an example—was approximately a month ago. We had a snowstorm much like this one, and a former mayor of the province found his way to the house just as we were finishing dinner.

ATTORNEY. It was a delicious meal. The poor man was unlucky to miss it. (*Crosses* U. L. *to buffet table.*)

PROSECUTOR. (*Crosses* D. L.) Unlucky in other ways too. He was convicted of poisoning his first wife. We sentenced him to hang.

TRAPP. (*Much amused at this.*) That would be enough to kill anyone's appetite.
PROSECUTOR. Naturally he was upset. But the law is the law—the sentence could not be set aside. (*Trapp gives Prosecutor a sharp look, half amused, half puzzled.*)
TRAPP. But didn't I read somewhere that capital punishment had recently been abolished in Switzerland?
PROSECUTOR. In Switzerland, yes. Not in our court.
JUDGE. (*Crosses to Trapp's* L. *shoulder at same time Attorney crosses to Trapp's* R. *shoulder, like a pincers movement.*) The mayor had the same notion. We tried to make him understand how necessary capital punishment is to the true spirit of our game. But he couldn't seem to grasp the point.
PROSECUTOR. He was generally a confused sort of man. Scarcely worth playing with.
ATTORNEY. Those are his trousers you're wearing, Mr. Trapp. He neglected to take them with him. (*Trapp roars with laughter. The others laugh too, but more quietly, and never taking their eyes off Trapp.*)
TRAPP. Well, I'm beginning to catch on. You want *me* to be the defendant, is that it?
ATTORNEY. Exactly! You'll make a *wonderful* defendant!
PROSECUTOR. (*Quietly. Crossing in to Trapp a step.*) It's the role for which you're best suited.
TRAPP. I wish I could agree with you. I'm a pretty respectable citizen, you know. No crimes, no secret vices, good credit rating. A few speeding tickets now and then, but otherwise my past is an open book.
PROSECUTOR. That is the type of book which sometimes yields the most interest.
JUDGE. We would be deeply grateful to you, Mr. Trapp. However, there's no obligation. We allow defendants to appear only on a voluntary basis.
TRAPP. What do I care about *that*? As long as you're asking me—
PROSECUTOR. (*Sharply. Crossing in another step.*) No. Don't make a hasty decision, Mr. Trapp. We have certain rigid rules. Once you've agreed to join us, you can't back out.
JUDGE. That's right. Once you place yourself under the juris-

diction of our court, you must submit to that jurisdiction right through to the end of the trial.

ATTORNEY. Otherwise, it wouldn't really *amount* to anything, you see.

TRAPP. Sure, I can see that all right. What's the point of playing a game if you're going to quit before the end?

PROSECUTOR. Exactly! You have a natural talent for our game, Mr. Trapp. It would be a pity not to make use of it.

OLD MAN. What do you say? Won't you please say yes? *(Pause. The four old men wait eagerly for Trapp's answer. He grins around at them, amused by the whole thing.)*

TRAPP. Are you gentlemen sure you want to play a game with me? I'm pretty good at games.—All right, I'll do it. *(There are cries of delight from the four old men. Prosecutor moves* U. L. *a few steps.)*

OLD MAN. *(Rising.)* He's going to do it! Everything's all right!

JUDGE. Mr. Trapp, on behalf of my colleagues and myself, I thank you.

ATTORNEY. It will be a pleasure for me to defend you, Mr. Trapp. I'm sure we'll put up a splendid fight, and win out in the end.

PROSECUTOR. I sincerely hope you have something to fight for —something really big.

JUDGE. *(Rising.)* Well now—I think we owe ourselves a treat, by way of celebration! We'll go out to the kitchen now for the final ritual—preparing the soufflé au liqueur. You must help, Gustave. You too, Joseph. *(Ushers them off* L. *and starts too.)*

TRAPP. *(Rising.)* Don't I get to go out to the kitchen with you? *(Judge stops.)*

JUDGE. I'm afraid not, Mr. Trapp. According to the rules the defendant is entitled to a private conference with his attorney before they appear in court.

ATTORNEY. We can't argue with the rules, Mr. Trapp.

JUDGE. We won't be long, Mr. Trapp. The game will commence along with the dessert. *(They exit* L., *leaving the Attorney with Trapp. Attorney goes over to kitchen door* L., *and shuts it tightly.)*

ATTORNEY. Just a small precaution. Gustave mustn't overhear our plans.

TRAPP. *(Amused. Goes to bar and refills his wine glass.)* This is all pretty anti-social, isn't it? Acting as if your friend were a Peeping Tom.

ATTORNEY. Peeping Tom?

TRAPP. A spy—a snooper.

ATTORNEY. (*Approaching Trapp.*) Ah, I understand. No, I don't suspect Gustave of being a Peeping Tom. He is the soul of honor. But it is dangerous to throw temptation in the way of any man, no matter how honorable he may be. (*Seats Trapp.*) Now then—we have only a limited amount of time, so let us proceed to matters of strategy. It would be best, I think, to confide your crime to me right now.

TRAPP. (*Puzzled.*) My crime?

ATTORNEY. Yes—the complete facts, if you please—so that the prosecutor won't catch us by surprise.

TRAPP. (*Doubtfully.*) Oh, come on, he's not going to catch me by surprise.

ATTORNEY. I see the direction of your thoughts, Mr. Trapp. You have observed our distinguished prosecutor. (*Crosses to* C.) You see that his hair is white—therefore you assume that he isn't really capable of performing his duties. (*Apologetically.*) Perhaps you assume the same thing about me.

TRAPP. No, not at all.

ATTORNEY. You're very tactful. Well, I won't speak for myself—but for my friend, Gustave, let me assure you that he is still in full command of his intellectual powers. He is not a man to be underestimated, and our host as well. The kindest, gentlest man on earth—when he's off the bench. But *on* the bench—just; severe; utterly impervious to emotional considerations.

TRAPP. (*Sitting at chess table,* C. *Grinning.*) You certainly throw yourself into this game, don't you?

ATTORNEY. (*Blushing.*) Well, I do give in to my feelings, I admit it.

TRAPP. I still don't see what you want me to do.

ATTORNEY. (*Crossing to* R. *of chess table.*) This is our standard procedure, Mr. Trapp: When court convenes you will announce what crime you wish to stand trial for—embezzlement, or wife-beating or blackmail—whatever little episode from your past presents the most promising possibilities. You will then plead not-guilty to this crime and it will be up to our friend, the prosecutor, to ferret out the proof, if he can. Now, as to your crime—

TRAPP. I hate to disappoint you—but it's just like I told all of you before. I haven't committed any crime. There isn't any episode from my past.

ATTORNEY. (*Crosses to* C. *again.*) Mr. Trapp—I'm your attorney. All communications between us are strictly confidential. I've seen abysses open, believe me.

TRAPP. (*Very good-humored about it.*) I'm sorry. I wish I could open an abyss for you now. But I guess I'm just innocent of any crime.

ATTORNEY. (*At chess table* C., *leans toward Trapp,* L. *More intently.*) Young man, listen to me—in this world of ours no one is completely innocent. Each of us carries some burden of guilt which troubles him and fills him with self loathing. I myself, when I was a very young man— (*Breaks off, moved.*) Where would sympathy, mercy, forgiveness come from if not for our common share of human fallibility? Such being the case, it would be very poor tactics to appear before our court without announcing exactly what crime you wish to be charged with.

TRAPP. And what would be good tactics?

ATTORNEY. To stand trial for some crime that isn't particularly shameful, but even rather admirable and charming—like swindling an insurance company, for instance. If the prosecutor *does* happen to stumble on the proof, I may be able to suggest that your guilt has a kind of nobility in it, that you gave the money to a widow or an orphan—robbing the rich to help the poor, so to speak.

TRAPP. That's very clever. The only trouble is, I *haven't* robbed the rich to help the poor. If you knew me better, you'd realize how completely out of character that is.

ATTORNEY. Perhaps so, Mr. Trapp. But you don't know our court. To maintain your innocence from the start, believe me, could easily be catastrophic. You'll be compelled, instead of choosing your own offense, to let one be thrust upon you.

TRAPP. Wait a second—I think I get you now. You want me to make up some imaginary crime, and pretend that I'm really—

ATTORNEY. (*Shocked.*) *That* would be perjury, Mr. Trapp! I'm certainly not urging you to commit perjury! I am merely suggesting that you can make it easier for everyone—

TRAPP. (*Slightly irritated.*) Why *should* I make it easy for you? I haven't committed any crime! If the prosecutor's so smart, let him find one!

ATTORNEY. He *will* find one. He excels at that. (*Gives up with a sigh.*) Very well, Mr. Trapp. I'm not in the habit of abandoning my clients merely because they don't see eye to eye with me. Only please listen to my advice on one matter—it is vitally important for you to weigh every word before you speak. The prosecutor will try very hard to trick you into saying the wrong thing.

TRAPP. A good salesman is never tricked into saying the wrong thing.

ATTORNEY. No doubt—but you have not yet exercised your salesmanship on Gustave Kummer. He is a dangerous adversary, Mr. Trapp. Please promise me to be frightened of him.

TRAPP. Sure, why not?

ATTORNEY. But will you *promise?*

TRAPP. All right, all right, I promise, I'll be frightened.

ATTORNEY. Then I will fetch my colleagues. (*He goes to kitchen door, turns and speaks feelingly.*) I'm counting on you, Mr. Trapp. (*He exits. Trapp is alone, rather amused. He takes a gulp of wine, and walks over to fireplace to see motif on the chimney. Nicole enters and starts cleaning up dishes. Trapp watches for a moment and then speaks.*)

TRAPP. You live here, do you?

NICOLE. No, I live in the village, Monsieur. I come here only when Monsieur Carpeau has guests.

TRAPP. (*Crossing* U. *to kitchen doorway.*) But you'll still be here later tonight, won't you? . . . After they've gone to bed?

NICOLE. (*Finishing up stacking tray at buffet table.*) Well, I have to clean up the kitchen, and turn down the beds. Sometimes this keeps me here until very late.

TRAPP. (*Propping his arm against the door, blocking her exit.*) And this will be one of those times?

NICOLE. (*Going as far as his arm.*) Have a pleasant evening, Monsieur. (*He finally smiles, raises his arm, and she leaves. Trapp goes back to the bar again for more wine. From the kitchen a procession appears, first the Judge, then Attorney, Prosecutor and Old Man.*)

ATTORNEY. Well, here we are.

JUDGE. What a lucky man you are, Mr. Trapp. So far you have tasted, as it were, only the minor works of Emile Carpeau. In a moment you'll have the unique opportunity of enjoying my masterpiece! (*He waves Pierre on. Pierre enters with a trayful of soufflé.*)

TRAPP. (*Rather startled, as he sees Pierre.*) Who's . . . he . . .?

JUDGE. Excuse me, Mr. Trapp, this is Pierre, my houseman, who lives here with me. He will serve us for the rest of the evening. He's a mute, but he isn't deaf. You can give him orders.

TRAPP. But what about the girl? (*Gesturing to kitchen. Crosses to above* L. C. *chair.*)

JUDGE. Oh, Nicole is never present when we play the game. She has her car outside. She will drive down to the village as soon as she is finished in the kitchen. (*Judge moves* U. C. *to serve soufflé. Pierre crosses to Judge* L. *to help him. Pierre puts two dishes on chess table, and gives one to Prosecutor, then stands in corner by kitchen door.*)

PROSECUTOR. (*Going up to Trapp.*) Well, Mr. Trapp, it looks as if you and I will be deadly enemies this evening. I may possibly say things about you which violate the ordinary rules of social behavior. But you understand, nothing personal will be meant. I apologize ahead of time.

TRAPP. (*Amused.*) Apologies accepted. (*The Prosecutor bows stiffly and goes to his seat, as the others have already done. The Attorney sits at chess table,* C. *Trapp goes to chess table, takes his dessert, and sits* U. R. *by book case.*)

JUDGE. (*Crossing to* C. *and eating his dessert.*) I'm terribly curious about what the defendant has in store for us. A beautiful stately confidence scheme perhaps? Or a quiet little tax fraud, notable for its classic simplicity.

ATTORNEY. (*Rising and going a step toward Trapp.*) I would like to satisfy your curiosity, Emile, but I'm afraid my client is a phenomenon of legal history. He's a defendant without a crime. He insists that he's innocent and leaves himself open to whatever charge the prosecutor may hit upon. (*A moment of startled silence, as the Judge frowns and the Prosecutor leans forward and gazes at Trapp intently, with a glint of satisfaction. Finally, the Old Man rises, crosses* D. C., *murmurs an eager question.*)

OLD MAN. He says that he's innocent? Is it really going to be one of those?

JUDGE. It would seem so, Joseph. (*Joseph crosses* D. *and sits in* D. L. *chair.*) Mr. Trapp, (*Crosses to* L. *of Trapp.*) I admire your courage. But you know, it isn't really necessary to impress us. As long as the trial hasn't started yet, you can still specify the crime for which you wish to be tried.

TRAPP. (*Rising and crossing* U. L. *to put empty plate on buffet.*) I keep telling you, there is no crime.
JUDGE. Bernard, you explained to him—?
ATTORNEY. With all the eloquence at my command.
JUDGE. (*Turning to Trapp.*) Well, then, Mr. Trapp, let me urge you once more—
PROSECUTOR. (*Breaking in sharply.*) Excuse me, Emile, but the defendant *is* over twenty-one. Presumably he knows how to take care of his own interests.
TRAPP. (*Crosses* D. *to* C.) I knew how to do *that* long before I was twenty-one. If we're going to have a game, let's make it a good one.
JUDGE. Very well. You leave me no alternative. The court will have to accept your decision. (*Crosses* L. *to* L. *chair.*) Mr. Prosecutor, you may begin the questioning.
TRAPP. But I didn't get up on the witness stand—I didn't swear to tell the truth and all that!
JUDGE. Our court doesn't go in for such formalities.
TRAPP. (*Backing a few steps* U. C. *Pointing to Pierre, standing guard at the door* R.) But *he's* still here! Don't tell me you let *him* play the game!
JUDGE. Pierre is one of our most important players. He's our combination bailiff, sheriff, and chief jailer. Well qualified because of his penal experience.
TRAPP. Penal experience? What penal experience?
ATTORNEY. Pierre spent ten years in prison, Mr. Trapp— (*Trapp crosses and sits.*) A certain merchant in the town took advantage of his little sister. It was a terrible thing. You couldn't blame Pierre for attacking the man.
PROSECUTOR. But the blow he struck was fatal, and I was obliged to prosecute him.
TRAPP. *You—?*
JUDGE. (*Crossing in to Trapp.*) And I sentenced him, Mr. Trapp.
ATTORNEY. (*With a sigh.*) Unfortunately I did not defend him.
TRAPP. (*With an uneasy look at Pierre, who has been listening to all this impassively.*) But under the circumstances—how could you hire him?
JUDGE. I was delighted to get him, Mr. Trapp. (*Crossing* U. *to Pierre.*) We're more than employer and employee—we're friends, we understand each other. There's nothing we wouldn't do for each

other. Isn't that right, Pierre? (*Pierre nods.*) Now then, if we might proceed with the questioning. (*Pierre goes up steps and sits on stool. Judge goes to above chess table. Joseph sits in* U. L. *chair.*)

TRAPP. Fine with me. Fire away.

PROSECUTOR. (*Crossing to* C. *Moves about room as he speaks.*) I understand you're a married man, Mr. Trapp.

TRAPP. Yes, I am.

PROSECUTOR. How long have you been married?

TRAPP. Eleven years.

PROSECUTOR. Have you any little ones?

TRAPP. (*Brightens up.*) Only one—Howard Junior. He's seven and a half. But he raises enough hell for quintuplets! Here. You want to see the latest picture? (*Takes out photograph. The old men admire it and pass it from one to the other.*)

JUDGE. A cheerful, sturdy young fellow. You're a lucky man, Mr. Trapp.

ATTORNEY. (*Looking at the picture and sighing.*) Children are the only true consolation in life, aren't they?

PROSECUTOR. (*Looking at the picture.*) A handsome boy, Mr. Trapp. If I may say so, he has your looks. (*Gives photo back to Trapp.*)

TRAPP. He's got brains, too. In New York, at the airport, when we said good-bye to him, he knew the names of all the planes, how many motors, and everything. We figure that he'll be a big scientist some day. That's where the money is.

PROSECUTOR. You left him in New York in the care of someone, I trust?

TRAPP. We left him with a governess.

PROSECUTOR. (*Watching Trapp closely.*) It seems a shame such a young boy should be separated from his parents.

ATTORNEY. (*Protesting.*) What else can Mr. Trapp do? He has to travel; it's his job.

PROSECUTOR. (*To Trapp, insinuatingly.*) And your wife's company is essential to your pleasure?

TRAPP. Sure. (*Prosecutor looks pleased, as if he had scored a point. Then Trapp goes on, smiling.*) But I begged her to stay in New York with the kid. (*Prosecutor reacts, annoyed.*) She was the one who insisted on coming with me. She's crazy about skiing, and Europeans— Well, if you're charging me with child neglect, Mr.

Prosecutor, you've got the wrong party. (*There is a moment of embarrassed silence. The wind is heard.*)

JUDGE. (*Crossing to fireplace with a significant glance at the Prosecutor.*) The storm seems to be growing worse, doesn't it? I'm afraid it's with us for the rest of the night.

PROSECUTOR. (*Crossing* U. *above chess table.*) Apparently the elements don't bother *you,* Mr. Trapp. The signs were sinister even this morning, yet you set off on your trip to Geneva anyway.

TRAPP. If you don't take chances you'll never get anything out of life.

PROSECUTOR. A healthy point of view, (*Crossing back to* C.) but I'm sure that your wife was terribly concerned for your safety when you said goodbye to her at the ski lodge.

TRAPP. Oh, she said she was . . . at first. But I told her there was a five thousand dollar commission at stake, and her concern disappeared fast enough.

PROSECUTOR. A five thousand dollar commission, you said? Tell me, Mr. Trapp—what type of merchandise do you sell?

TRAPP. I'm not dealing in anything illegal, if that's what you're wondering. I'm the exclusive agent in Europe for Haphaeston.

JUDGE. Haphaeston? The name is unfamiliar to me.

TRAPP. (*Automatically going into his sales talk, almost in manner of a circus barker. Rising, crosses to* C.) It's the new miracle textile—tear-proof, water-proof, tough but transparent, (*Judge sits.*) as useful in industry as in the world of fashion, in war as in peace; the ideal material for parachutes, and at the same time most enticing in milady's nightgown— (*He laughs and the others join in—all except the Defense Attorney.*)

PROSECUTOR. (*Crossing* D. *to Trapp's* R. *Insinuatingly.*) As you know from personal research?

ATTORNEY. On his wife's nightgown!

TRAPP. (*Smiling.*) That's right.

PROSECUTOR. (*Annoyed again, but covering it.*) Bravo, Mr. Trapp. I can see why you're the company's exclusive agent. I'm ready to give you an order for Haphaeston right now.

TRAPP. Orders are always cheerfully accepted. (*Sits.*)

PROSECUTOR. (*Crossing* U. C.) But tell me—am I right in assuming, from various remarks you've made, that you weren't always the successful man we see before us tonight?

ATTORNEY. Careful, careful.

TRAPP. Well, he's right about that, you know. I wasn't born with a silver spoon in my mouth. (*Crosses* U. *to behind chess table.*) In his whole lifetime my old man never made as much money as I make in one year. (*A bit more firmly. Pours himself another glass of wine from bar.*) Well, it's a hell of a lot different for *my* boy, I can tell you *that.*

PROSECUTOR. In short, you've worked hard to get where you are today?

TRAPP. Damned hard, and I'm not too modest to say so.

PROSECUTOR. (*Small circle* U. *and* R., *turning half back.*) Admirable, most admirable. And your educational background?

TRAPP. (*With great pride.*) The school of hard knocks.

PROSECUTOR. (*Very dryly.*) Oh yes, I've heard of it. But could you be more specific?

TRAPP. Second year high school, that's as far as I got. The old man died and I went to work in the real estate business.

PROSECUTOR. You became an office boy with a real estate firm?

TRAPP. Who, me? *That's* no way to get anywhere! I knew this fellow who used to snap up small pieces of property that the city was planning to buy—he had a friend in City Hall who gave him the tips.

PROSECUTOR. But I don't quite see what *your* duties were.

TRAPP. After a while, you see, my boss got too well known, so he used me to do the buying for him. I was young and innocent looking, you see.

ATTORNEY. (*Breaking in quickly. Rising.*) You were too young to know that you were doing anything wrong, Mr. Trapp? Perhaps this is the crime you'd like to be charged with.

TRAPP. (*Mockingly, to Prosecutor.*) Yeah, I'll let you try me for that. (*Sits back in chair* L. *of chess table.*)

PROSECUTOR. (*Crossing* D. L. *to Judge. Not grabbing the bait.*) Excuse me, your Honor, but that decision is no longer in Mr. Trapp's hands.

JUDGE. Quite so. Go on with the questioning.

PROSECUTOR. (*Crossing back to* C.) Mr. Trapp, you've referred to your father. But what of your mother? Is she still alive?

TRAPP. I'm afraid not. She died a couple of years ago.

PROSECUTOR. I'm sorry. But at least you were able to make her last years happy and comfortable.

TRAPP. (*Smiling a little.*) You're right, I was able to do that. I set her up in a nice little apartment—on Central Park South.
PROSECUTOR. What a consolation it is to us when our dear ones are able to die happy.
TRAPP. (*A shadow over his face.*) Well—
PROSECUTOR. (*Gently.*) She didn't die happy, Mr. Trapp?
TRAPP. (*Bitterly.*) She would have if it hadn't been for my brothers.
PROSECUTOR. Your brothers aren't as successful as you?
TRAPP. They never *could* earn a decent living! That's why they were always pressuring *her* to get money out of *me!* I was supposed to go broke taking care of Frank's baby and Harry's business!
PROSECUTOR. I gather you held firm against their unfair tactics?
TRAPP. Of course I did. Nobody makes a sucker out of *me.* (*More softly.*) Mama could never understand it, though. "They're your own brothers," she kept saying—and she used to slip them money when she thought I didn't know about it.
PROSECUTOR. But how could you prevent her from giving them money, Mr. Trapp, unless you stopped her allowance?
ATTORNEY. Watch out.
TRAPP. Sorry, Mr. Prosecutor. I shut my eyes to the whole thing. I supported her to the end. (*Rising, crosses* D. *far* R.)
JUDGE. Pierre, the coffee. (*Pierre exits through kitchen door,* L.)
TRAPP. (*Aside to Attorney.*) We're doing great, aren't we? I told you I was good at games. (*Prosecutor gets brandy and glass from bar.*)
ATTORNEY. (*Crossing* D. *to him.*) You're doing much too well. I don't like it. You're getting overconfident.
TRAPP. All right, all right. Now relax, will you. Let me enjoy the game. Don't be a spoil-sport.
PROSECUTOR. (*Coming up to Trapp with brandy.*) Before we resume, perhaps Mr. Trapp would prefer something a little more stimulating than coffee. Some of this fine old cognac for instance.
TRAPP. That's a good idea.
ATTORNEY. (*Uneasily.*) Don't you think coffee would be better for you, Mr. Trapp? You must keep a clear head, you know.
TRAPP. Listen, I guess I know how to hold my liquor (*Pierre*

enters with coffee.) after all these years. (*Accepts cognac from Prosecutor.*)

PROSECUTOR. Well, shall we return to the real estate business?

TRAPP. Not much chance of that, I'm glad to say. (*Sits. As questioning goes on, Pierre serves the old men, then resumes standing guard at door,* L.)

PROSECUTOR. (*With a thin smile.*) In memory only, of course. Let us compare the two pictures—Howard Trapp, the young boy, obscure, uneducated, struggling against poverty; and Howard Trapp, the grown man, thriving, prosperous, the exclusive European sales agent for the king of artificial fabrics. A striking contrast, isn't it? (*Assuming a confidential manner.*) Just between us, my dear sir—you've bulldozed your way up rather quickly, haven't you?

TRAPP. (*Responding in the same confidential manner.*) Damned right I have. (*He reaches out for the brandy bottle, which Prosecutor has placed on chess table,* C. *The Attorney makes an attempt to pull it away but Trapp gets it first and refills his glass. He holds on to the bottle.*) Ten years ago I was just another traveling salesman—wearing out my shoes for two-bit commissions. And today—well, do any of *you* own two English sports cars?

PROSECUTOR. Two English sports cars! That's amazing.

ATTORNEY. Why amazing? They're very small cars.

PROSECUTOR. How did you do it, Mr. Trapp? Was it simply diligence and hard work?

TRAPP. (*Laughing, very self-satisfied. Rising and crossing to above table.*) Oh no, it wasn't that easy. I could've been the most diligent salesman who ever lived, but I still had to get around Foster, and believe me that was tough.

PROSECUTOR. Oh, and who is this Mr. Foster? (*Sits in chair* L. *of table.*)

TRAPP. He was the European sales agent before me. A few years ago I was his chief assistant—stuck in the New York office, not even an expense account.

PROSECUTOR. And you say that you had to get him out of the way?

ATTORNEY. I object to the prosecutor's choice of words.

PROSECUTOR. I'll re-frame the question. You say that Mr. Foster is no longer in the way?

TRAPP. I certainly wouldn't be here now if he *was*.

PROSECUTOR. How lucky for you then that he decided to step down.

TRAPP. (*Laughs smugly.*) I guess you can call it luck.

PROSECUTOR. You're smiling with pleasure, no doubt, at the thought of your former chief enjoying the fruits of his labor at some resort hotel, basking at this moment in the sunshine, surrounded by delicious girls!

TRAPP. (*Laughs. Crossing to* C.) I don't know what he's surrounded by—though I could make a good guess. The fact is, he died five years ago.

ATTORNEY. (*Jumping up.*) Your honor, would you please instruct the witness that he needn't answer any questions before consulting with his attorney.

JUDGE. I so instruct you, Mr. Trapp. (*Attorney sits.*) You ought to be more discreet, you know, when dangerous questions are put to you.

PROSECUTOR. (*Rising and crossing* D. L. *to Judge.*) With all respect, your honor, I cannot admit that my question was dangerous. Dangerous is an improper word.

JUDGE. With all respect, Mr. Prosecutor, I will not be lectured on my choice of language in my own court.

PROSECUTOR. I beg your honor's pardon.

TRAPP. (*Taking pleasure in the imbroglio.*) Well, I don't see what everybody's getting so excited about. I was just telling the simple facts.

PROSECUTOR. (*Crossing back to* C.) And how sad those simple facts are. Mr. Foster died five years ago. One can't help feeling sorry for the poor old gentleman.

TRAPP. He wasn't so old. Fifty-two, to be exact.

PROSECUTOR. In the prime of life! This story grows sadder and sadder. First he retires from his job, and then, before he has a chance to savor his leisure, he dies.

TRAPP. No, you've got it the wrong way round. He died while he was still working for the company. It was *after* he died that I took his place. (*There is a long silence at this. The Attorney sits back with a sigh of despair. The Judge frowns. The Old Man peers at Trapp curiously, the Prosecutor smiles with satisfaction.*)

PROSECUTOR. Your honor, fortune smiles upon us. I submit that we no longer have a defendant without a crime. We've done a little digging, and lo and behold! We've come up with a corpse. The prosecution now formally charges the defendant with murder.

TRAPP. Murder—?

PROSECUTOR. The murder of his former chief, the late Mr. Foster. Murder in the first degree.

ATTORNEY. (*Rising to his feet indignantly.*) Your honor, I object! The prosecutor has pulled this absurd charge right out of the air.

JUDGE. The charge does come as something of a surprise, Mr. Prosecutor.

PROSECUTOR. I'll be happy to justify it, your honor. (*Crossing* D. L. *to Judge.*) One—a man has died. Two—the defendant admits that he had a motive for this man's death. (*Back* U. C., *opposite Trapp.*) Three—the defendant has revealed a distinct absence of regret for this man's death; indeed, he has revealed a definite satisfaction. Four—the prosecution firmly believes in the guilt of this defendant and stakes its legal reputation on its ability to prove that guilt. (*Trapp puts down his glass on chess table in amazement.*)

ATTORNEY. The prosecutor's monumental self-confidence is hardly evidence.

PROSECUTOR. (*Crossing* D. R. C. *to Attorney.*) Surely my past record in this court is not irrelevant to the argument. (*Crosses* L. *to Judge.*) I have a nose for these things, as you all know. I *smell* this crime, your honor. I feel that the ends of justice would be thwarted if this defendant weren't bound over for trial.

JUDGE. But you'll be fighting against great odds. If you fail to substantiate the charge, you'll seriously damage your reputation in this court.

PROSECUTOR. I'm willing to accept that risk, your honor.

ATTORNEY. His willingness is beside the point.

JUDGE. No, I don't think it is. The prosecutor's nose cannot be entirely ignored. The charge of murder in the first degree is hereby accepted. (*Prosecutor returns to his chair, near dining table,* U. L.)

TRAPP. (*Crossing* D. C.) But I haven't murdered anybody. Don't you think you're carrying the joke a little too far?

JUDGE. (*Rising and walking over to face Trapp.*) Murder is no joke, Mr. Trapp. It is so grave a charge indeed that it clearly cannot be tried in this friendly informal atmosphere. We require a rearrangement of the physical accoutrements more suited to the nature of the proceedings. Joseph, I'll leave you to take care of that, while the prosecutor, the defense attorney, and I retire to our respective rooms to put on our robes of office. Pierre, please help Monsieur Pillet. (*Pierre starts clearing away the coffee things. The Judge, Prosecutor, and Attorney rise and move solemnly to the door* R. *Trapp stares at them.*)

TRAPP. But why all this hocus-pocus? Why do you need robes of office?

PROSECUTOR. (*Quietly, with significance.*) It's necessary, Mr. Trapp. (*They all exit into the foyer* R., *then start up the stairs. Trapp shakes his head, bewildered, then turns to the Old Man who is rising to his feet.*)

TRAPP. (*Rising.*) Mr. Pillet, won't they let you have a robe of office, too?

OLD MAN. Oh no. As soon as I rearrange the physical accoutrements, I'll be leaving. (*Opens drape.*)

TRAPP. You mean, you won't be here for the rest of the game? (*Pierre exits to the kitchen* L., *with tray and coffee things.*)

OLD MAN. Oh no, it wouldn't be seemly. It wouldn't be in good taste. Now that we have a case of murder, a capital crime—well, for the sake of your feelings . . . (*Starts going about his business.*)

TRAPP. What've my feelings got to do with it?

OLD MAN. Didn't anybody tell you? Dear me, you should have been told. I'm not a lawyer, Mr. Trapp. For twenty-five years I served the municipality as its official hangman. (*Trapp stares at the Old Man, shocked and horrified. But the Old Man is blandly unaware of the effect he's produced. Goes to chess table to put bottle and glasses on the bar. The curtain falls.*)

END OF ACT ONE

ACT II

SCENE 1

Five minutes later, the furniture slightly rearranged, the room produces a sinister courtroom effect. Pierre is just finishing the arranging. The Old Man supervises him, while Trapp stands aside, watching them, agitated and bewildered.

OLD MAN. Yes, that's fine, Pierre. Now I'll go up and tell them we're ready. (*The Old Man goes upstairs* R. *Pierre continues to arrange furniture. Trapp watches him, hesitates, then goes up to him.*)

TRAPP. Just a minute, will you. (*Pierre stops and smiles expectantly. Conscious of being too agitated, Trapp forces himself to put on a very casual manner.*) I wanted to ask you something— Pierre, that's your name, isn't it? (*He pauses, as if for encouragement, but Pierre just waits amiably. Trapp clears his throat, then continues.*) About this game of theirs—you've watched them play it often, haven't you? (*Pierre nods.*) The last time, for instance— there was a stranger who came here just like me, wasn't there? A mayor of the province, they said. (*Pierre nods and briefly pantomimes the protruding waistline, puffed-out cheeks, and pompous manner of the Mayor. Then he laughs. Trapp laughs too, but tensely.*) That's right, that's who I mean. When the mayor played this game of theirs that night—did they go in for this same hocus-pocus? (*Pierre looks puzzled.*) I mean, did they fix up the rooms like this? (*Pierre nods.*) I see. (*Thinking hard.*) And after the game was over—the next morning, I mean— (*Trap can't keep a certain anxiety out of his voice as he comes to the important question.*) —when the mayor came down for breakfast—everybody had a big laugh over the game, didn't they? (*Pierre nods. Trapp grabs at this straw eagerly.*) They did? In other words, the mayor was in a good mood—when he left the house? (*Pierre's smile fades. He looks puzzled. Then he shakes his head, frowning. In spite of himself, Trapp raises his voice, alarmed.*) The mayor *wasn't* in a good mood when he left the house? (*Pierre grins. His voice shaking, Trapp jumps to the next inevitable question.*) What are you grinning about? You mean the mayor *didn't* leave the house? (*Pierre still smiles and nods. Trapp gives a grin of relief.*) Then he *did* leave the house—you saw him go? (*Pierre nods, still more energetically, and smiles broadly. Trapp can hardly hide his relief.*) You saw him go! Thanks a lot, Pierre! I mean, thanks! (*Pierre laughs a knowing, almost mischievous laugh, and exits* L. *Trapp's relieved look changes to one of alarm and uncertainty again. He calls after Pierre.*) Wait a second! What are you grinning at? Come back here— (*No answer. Upset, Trapp hurries to the brandy on mantel. Then he paces in agitation. Nicole comes out of the kitchen. She is no longer in her maid's uniform. She carries a coat and wears hat, boots, and is rather smartly dressed. Seeing Trapp, she knocks on the kitchen door jamb.*) Yes?

NICOLE. (*Coming into the room.*) I thought Monsieur Carpeau . . .

TRAPP. He went upstairs.

NICOLE. (*Crossing* R. *to bottom step.*) I wanted to tell him that I'm leaving now.

TRAPP. How can you leave? That snow . . .

NICOLE. I have great experience driving in this weather.

TRAPP. (*Gesturing out window.*) Was that your car by the front gate, I saw when I came in?

NICOLE. Yes. Well, I'll go up to Monsieur Carpeau. (*She starts up the steps. Trapp takes a step after her, and there is a note of urgency in his voice.*)

TRAPP. No. Don't go.

NICOLE. (*Turning, puzzled.*) Monsieur?

TRAPP. (*Getting a hold of himself.*) Why don't you hang around until the old gentlemen have gone to bed?

NICOLE. (*Assuming her coquettish manner.*) Why should I, Monsieur?

TRAPP. We could have a drink together.

NICOLE. I never drink before I drive down the mountain.

TRAPP. Okay, we'll just talk.

NICOLE. And what will we talk about? (*Putting her coat down.*)

TRAPP. Who knows? Politics, life, (*He comes up to her step.*) . . . Swiss-American relations. I'm a very interesting conversationalist.

NICOLE. (*Stepping away from him, smiling sweetly.*) Will we talk about your wife, Monsieur?

TRAPP. (*Crossing* D. R.) My wife . . . ? (*Grins.*) Let's stick to pleasant subjects.

NICOLE. (*Crossing* D. C.) For most men it *is* a pleasure to talk about their wives.

TRAPP. (*Crossing* R. *to bar.*) Most men aren't on the verge of getting a divorce.

NICOLE. Oh, I'm so sorry.

TRAPP. Don't be. Helen's just as happy about it as I am.

NICOLE. Yet you travel together, you stay at the same hotel?

TRAPP. Have to keep up appearances. A certain business contact over here doesn't approve of divorces. So, soon as I land this deal I'm working on, Helen and I will call it quits. (*Softer, more insinuating.*) Meanwhile, life has to go on, doesn't it? (*He moves very close to her, touching her cheek with the back of his finger.*) Helen hasn't stopped enjoying herself, so why should I?

NICOLE. (*Moving a step away from him.*) Very well. We won't bring your wife into the conversation.

TRAPP. (*Encouraged, stepping close to her again, and starting to put his arm around her waist.*) Then we *are* going to have a conversation?

NICOLE. (*Sliding from his grasp, and crossing* U. R. *to get her coat.*) I will sit awhile in the kitchen. When you're finished for the evening, knock on the door. Perhaps I will still be here. (*She crosses to the kitchen door.*)

TRAPP. I won't be long, that's for sure!

NICOLE. (*Turning to him.*) When Monsieur Carpeau and his friends play their game, they are often at it until early morning.

TRAPP. (*Coming to her.*) Are they? About this game. . . .

NICOLE. (*Breaking in.*) I must go now. (*She turns, but Trapp stops her, with his hand on her arm.*)

TRAPP. You'll be in the kitchen, when I get through here?

NICOLE. (*With a mischievous smile.*) I have said "perhaps."

TRAPP. Be there . . . please. (*The Prosecutor comes down the stairs, with a book in his hand, and enters the living room* R.)

PROSECUTOR. Mr. Trapp? (*Trapp whirls around with a cry of surprise.*) I'm so sorry—I didn't mean to startle you.

NICOLE. (*Startled.*) Good night, Monsieur. (*Exits.*)

TRAPP. (*Getting himself under control.*) Well—look at you. You look like you're about to graduate from college.

PROSECUTOR. My robe of office, you mean? Yes, it *is* just a trifle pompous. (*Crossing to* R. *of lectern, and putting the book on it.*) For myself, I could easily do without these outward forms and symbols—but experience has taught us that they're necessary to establish the proper note of solemnity.

TRAPP. (*Crossing* D. C.) You know, I'm just beginning to get the idea of this game of yours. You get hold of some outsider like me, talk about murders and hangmen and the "proper note of solemnity," and pretty soon you have him scared to death! I have to hand it to you, I nearly fell for it! (*Pick up brandy bottle and glass, pours.*)

PROSECUTOR. I'm glad it interests you, Mr. Trapp. It's most gratifying to feel that our guest is having an enjoyable evening.

TRAPP. (*Jovially.*) Well, when do we start? Where's everybody else?

PROSECUTOR. (*Crossing* L. *to opposite Trapp at table.*) I hurried a bit, so that I might talk to you for a moment. A confidential matter in connection with the case. I prefer to talk to you alone, but if you express a wish for your attorney—

TRAPP. My attorney? Oh, I get it—the "proper note of solemnity" again. No thank you. I'll talk to you without my attorney. I've got nothing to be afraid of. (*Sits* L. *of table.*)

PROSECUTOR. I admire that attitude, Mr. Trapp. Others might dismiss it as foolhardiness, but I call it courage. (*Pulls out chair from* L. *table, and sits on arm, facing Trapp.*) Nevertheless, the wise man tempers courage with prudence, doesn't he? As I sincerely ask you to do now.

TRAPP. I don't think I know what you mean.

PROSECUTOR. I offer you the opportunity to plead guilty to murder in the second degree. If you change your plea, the prosecution is prepared to press for the appropriate reduction of your sentence. Thus you can avoid the supreme penalty.

TRAPP. Wait a second—let me get this straight. I'm supposed to cop a plea—like they say in the movies?

PROSECUTOR. I believe that *is* the expression.

TRAPP. You know, I'll bet there's a million dollars in this game of yours!

PROSECUTOR. How so?
TRAPP. If somebody put it out commercially, I mean. With a board, and markers, and a pair of dice. "You decide to cop a plea—go to jail and miss your turn."
PROSECUTOR. (*Smiling amiably.*) I see. And the winner is the first player who reaches the hangman's noose.
TRAPP. Exactly! That's the spirit of it! (*Rising, dumps ashtray butts into fire, then returns to seat.*) You know, sometimes you and your friends actually talk as if you're not completely off your rockers.
PROSECUTOR. Rockers? A colloquial term for rocking-chairs, isn't it?
TRAPP. A colloquial term for not exactly all there— (*Touching his head with his finger.*)
PROSECUTOR. Ah! I follow you! You suspect us of being mentally unstable, do you? An interesting point of view. (*Rising, crosses* D. C., *staring out front.*) How does one answer such an accusation? Perhaps we *are* insane in a sense. Perhaps every man is insane who believes deeply in an idea and does everything in his power to carry it out. (*Crossing back* L., *looking at Trapp across table.*) Now Mr. Trapp, since we haven't too much time—how do you react to my offer?
TRAPP. To plead guilty? Not a chance. You wouldn't really want me to, would you?
PROSECUTOR. I admit it, Mr. Trapp. I'm not sorry you turned me down. There's something a bit tepid, insipid even, about second degree murder. For a real challenge, give me first degree every time. My compliments. You're a true sportsman. (*Trapp rises and bows. The Judge and the Attorney enter the living-room* R. *The Old Man takes a seat in the foyer* R., *Prosecutor crosses to* R. *of lectern.*)
JUDGE. Very sorry to keep you waiting, Mr. Trapp.
TRAPP. That's all right, your honor. I'm really looking forward to the next round.
JUDGE. Excellent, excellent. (*Pierre returns,* L., *and takes up place by living room door,* R.)
ATTORNEY. (*Crossing* D. R. *across lectern from Prosecutor.*) For heaven's sake, Gustave, don't make such long speeches tonight. Twice in the last year the trial has dragged on until two o'clock

in the morning. If you remember, by the time we convicted that female novelist from Sweden, she was already fast asleep. *Some* of us are obliged to get our rest, you know.

JUDGE. (*Rapping with gavel.*) Gentlemen, court will now convene.

PROSECUTOR. Your honor, I would like the defendant to take the stand. (*Attorney crosses* L. *to table, then around to Judge.*)

ATTORNEY. Your honor, I move that these entire proceedings be declared a mis-trial, and that the defendant be immediately discharged.

PROSECUTOR. (*Coming in a couple of steps.*) Your honor, the defense attorney's theatrical trickery is most—

ATTORNEY. (*Crosses to Prosecutor.*) I am not indulging in theatrical trickery! (*Crosses back to Judge.*) I deeply resent the prosecutor's insinuation!

JUDGE. Gentlemen! The defense attorney has made a motion. The court will hear his arguments—without interruption.

ATTORNEY. I move for a mis-trial, on the grounds that the prosecution has been tampering with a witness. While your honor and I were out of the courtroom, putting on our robes of office, the prosecutor conducted a private conference with the witness, (*Crossing* D. *to Trapp's* L. *shoulder.*) Howard Trapp. That's correct, isn't it, Mr. Trapp?

TRAPP. Sure, we had a talk—

PROSECUTOR. Your honor, this charge would be insulting if it weren't laughable. In a murder trial the defendant is always available for questioning by the authorities.

ATTORNEY. But the defendant has no legal obligation to answer questions.

PROSECUTOR. (*Crossing* L. C. *to Trapp.*) Mr. Trapp spoke to me voluntarily. Isn't that so, M. Trapp?

TRAPP. (*Following the argument with amusement.*) That's a fact.

ATTORNEY. Even so, the defendant has the right to undergo such an examination in the presence of his own attorney.

PROSECUTOR. Mr. Trapp, did I or did I not inform you of that right?

TRAPP. You sure did.

PROSECUTOR. And what was your decision?

TRAPP. I decided to talk to you alone. Why not?

ATTORNEY. Mr. Trapp, was I present when you made this decision?

TRAPP. Of course not.

ATTORNEY. No arguments were advanced, then, as to why you *shouldn't* talk to the prosecutor alone?

TRAPP. He asked me, and I said yes. What else do you want?

ATTORNEY. Nothing whatever, Mr. Trapp. (*Crossing* U. C. *to Judge.*) Your honor, the case is clear. Obviously the defendant was deprived of his rights—and the fact that he himself co-operated in this deprivation hardly makes it less flagrant.

PROSECUTOR. (*Crossing to* R. C.) Excuse me, your honor. It must be shown that I exercised undue influence *on the defendant.* I offered him a chance to plead guilty to second-degree murder—he refused the offer—and that was that.

ATTORNEY. The prosecutor apparently expects us to forget that he is a master in the art of pushing witnesses sub-consciously in one direction or another.

PROSECUTOR. That's arrant nonsense! (*Trapp, amused, rises and crosses to* L. *proscenium, watching.*)

ATTORNEY. (*Crosses to prosecutor.*) I'm not surprised to hear the prosecutor describe the ethical basis of our court as nonsense. What can we expect from one who puts convictions above human rights?

PROSECUTOR. The defense attorney's remark was inexcusable. It isn't difficult to understand why the streets of Geneva are packed with criminals who have cheated the law!

ATTORNEY. Nor is it difficult to understand why the cemeteries are filled with the innocent victims of cold inhuman logic!

JUDGE. (*Rapping, angrily.*) Gentlemen, stop this at once! (*Prosecutor and Attorney fall silent, glaring at each other. Trapp grins and shakes his head.*)

TRAPP. Don't stop the fight now, Judge. It was just getting interesting.

JUDGE. I cannot allow such displays of emotionalism in my court. Now as to the defense's motion—the final determination must rest with the defendant himself. Mr. Trapp, do you feel that the prosecutor used undue pressure or influence on you? (*Prosecutor and Attorney turn anxiously to Trapp.*)

TRAPP. (*Crossing up to kitchen door.*) If I say yes, that's the end of the game, isn't it?

JUDGE. It is. I will be obliged to dismiss the case.

TRAPP. (*Pause, smiling.*) Hell, I've never lost a game in my life. The answer is definitely no. (*The Prosecutor smirks. The Attorney sighs.*)

ATTORNEY. People who won't let themselves be helped (*Crosses* D. *to Prosecutor.*) —! (*Smiles at Prosecutor.*) Well, I tried, didn't I, Gustave?

PROSECUTOR. A valiant effort, Bernard—you nearly routed me ignominiously. (*Trapp picks up his glass and bottle, pouring.*) Mr. Trapp, will you please take the stand. (*Attorney crosses* L. *to his seat* L. *of table. Motioning at the raised chair next to the bench* L. *Trapp nods cheerfully and starts up to the chair showing by his slight swaying motion that he is already fairly drunk. He carries the bottle.*)

JUDGE. Excuse me, Mr. Trapp, you'll have to leave your glass.

TRAPP. I haven't finished my drink.

JUDGE. Circumstances have changed. I regret it, but—

PROSECUTOR. Your honor, couldn't the ruling be suspended on this one occasion? The defendant seems to be unusually dependent on this source of sustenance.

ATTORNEY. (*On his feet.*) I see absolutely no reason to suspend the ruling, your honor!

TRAPP. Say, whose side are you on anyway?

ATTORNEY. Yours, Mr. Trapp—which is more than I can say for you. That's why I think it advisable for you to stop drinking.

TRAPP. But I need the sustenance. After all, a man doesn't stand trial for murder every day of his life.

PROSECUTOR. Seldom more than once, Mr. Trapp.

JUDGE. (*Rapping his gavel, then turning to Trapp.*) I cannot allow you to keep the glass, Mr. Trapp.

TRAPP. It's only a game, isn't it?

JUDGE. The bailiff will please relieve the defendant of his glass. (*Pierre approaches Trapp quietly but relentlessly. Trapp holds out a moment longer, then shoves the bottle at Pierre, who replaces it on the mantel.*)

TRAPP. Okay, okay— What difference does it make? (*Crosses to witness chair [*R. *of table] and sits. Prosecutor steps up to Trapp, smiling amiably.*)

PROSECUTOR. Well now—why don't you save us all a lot of

time and effort, Mr. Trapp? Why don't you tell us how you killed the late Foster?

TRAPP. But I didn't kill him.

PROSECUTOR. He's dead, is he not?

TRAPP. Yes.

PROSECUTOR. His death provided you with the job you wanted, didn't it?

TRAPP. So what? Whenever a man dies *somebody* gets something out of it. So, do you automatically call it murder? At that rate you'd be putting half the world on trial.

PROSECUTOR. We're *not* putting half the world on trial, Mr. Trapp—it's your guilt alone that concerns us. Now why not make a clean breast of it and throw yourself on the mercy of the court? It often leads to a mitigation of the punishment, you know.

TRAPP. But I didn't murder anybody! I refuse to accept *any* punishment!

JUDGE. (*Gently, but firmly.*) You're in no position to refuse or accept. That is in the discretion of the court.

TRAPP. (*Jumping up, moving* U. C. *to Judge.*) The court! I don't give a damn about—

ATTORNEY. (*Rising.*) Tch, tch, Mr. Trapp, Mr. Trapp . . .

TRAPP. (*Pause.*) Sorry, gentlemen—no intention of spoiling the game. On with the questions. (*Sits back in witness chair.*)

PROSECUTOR. Mr. Trapp, did you poison the late Foster?

TRAPP. (*Very irritated.*) Don't be ridiculous.

PROSECUTOR. (*Driving.*) Well, shall we say that you strangled him?

TRAPP. Wrong again.

PROSECUTOR. You secretly arranged a traffic accident?

TRAPP. (*Raising his voice, putting on a desperate manner.*) All right, (*Jumping up, coming a few steps* D.) all right—I can't hold out any longer—I'll confess! I killed him!

ATTORNEY. (*Rising.*) Mr. Trapp, for heaven's sake! Your honor, I insist that you tell the witness—

TRAPP. (*Coming* U. C.) No, no, don't tell me anything! My conscience is bothering me too much—I *have* to talk!

JUDGE. (*Troubled.*) You're under no obligation, Mr. Trapp—

TRAPP. (U. *to Judge.*) I want to, I want to!

PROSECUTOR. (*With a puzzled look.*) Then tell us how you committed the murder, Mr. Trapp.

TRAPP. (*In a low intense voice, making a big dramatic production out of his story. A long pause, then he slowly turns and comes* D. C. *during the course of this speech.*) I went to Foster's office that morning. I knocked on the door. He said, "Come in." I went in. He said to me, "Trapp, there's an error in this report you just submitted." (*Breaks off with a shudder.*)

PROSECUTOR. (*Eagerly, leaning forward.*) Go on, go on!

TRAPP. (*In the same low, intense voice. Sitting.*) I said to him, "Mr. Foster, thank you for pointing it out to me. And since you've been kind enough to do part of my work for me—I'm going to turn this week's salary check over to you." (*Trapp lifts his head and blurts out his final words triumphantly.*) And it turned out just exactly as I planned! He dropped dead of the shock! (*The Judge, Attorney and Prosecutor gape with surprise, and Trapp bursts into loud laughter. It is a few moments before he can control his amusement.*) He fell for it! (*Prosecutor, glaring, sits* R. *of his lectern.*) He really fell for it! (*Rises, crosses to Prosecutor* R.) Well, that'll show you, Mr. Prosecutor! You're not the only one who can pull the wool over people's eyes! (*He is convulsed with laughter again. Gradually the old men recover their powers of speech. The Attorney shakes his head.*)

ATTORNEY. Mr. Trapp—you mustn't—you really mustn't do things like that! I'm not a young man any more, you know.

PROSECUTOR. (*Coldly.*) Mr. Trapp—you *did* pull the wool over my eyes—and brilliantly too. For that I congratulate you. (*Trapp starts toward his chair, is stopped short.*) But for your utter disregard of courtroom decorum—

JUDGE. (*Quiet but very angry.*) Excuse me, Mr. Prosecutor, but *I* will deliver the admonitions here. (*Waits till they fall silent and turn to him.*) Mr. Trapp, (*Trapp crosses* U. *to Judge.*) this interlude has been most amusing, no doubt, but you apparently fail to realize that you are standing trial for murder. I must warn you here and now that no further exhibition of levity will be tolerated by the court.

TRAPP. (*Long pause. Embarrassed by their solemn silence.*) Well, I'm sorry— (*Crosses* D. C.) If I thought you were going to get so upset—I was only trying to pump a little fun into the game. (*Sits. His voice trails off uncertainly.*)

JUDGE. (*Gravely.*) The questioning will proceed.

PROSECUTOR. (*Rising, crossing to* C.) Well now, Mr. Trapp— I'd like to get back to the subject of the late Foster's murder.

TRAPP. Too bad, Mr. Prosecutor. All kidding aside, there wasn't any murder. The old gangster died of a heart attack.

PROSECUTOR. The old gangster?

TRAPP. Just a name we had for him in the office. Sort of a joke— because some people thought he was too much of a tyrant, always bossing people around, never giving them credit for their work. Actually he wasn't such a bad guy— I guess it was a pretty stupid joke.

PROSECUTOR. I see. Now you were telling us about his heart attack. (*The Prosecutor moves about near witness stand as he speaks. Does so throughout his interrogation of Trapp.*)

TRAPP. It wasn't his first. He had two or three in his last few years. Pretended to be perfectly healthy, of course—kind of proud and sensitive I guess— But the fact is, every shock was dangerous.

PROSECUTOR. He hid this scrupulously from his business associates?

TRAPP. Nobody in the office even suspected it.

PROSECUTOR. (*Driving just a bit harder.*) Then how did *you* happen to know it?

TRAPP. Oh, I found out from the most reliable possible source.

PROSECUTOR. Which was?

TRAPP. I found out from his wife.

PROSECUTOR. From his wife.

ATTORNEY. (*To Trapp, in an urgent undertone.*) Go slowly, go slowly.

PROSECUTOR. You were on friendly terms with the late Foster's wife?

TRAPP. (*A little cautiously.*) Sure—we were friends.

PROSECUTOR. You were *close* friends?

TRAPP. I don't know what you mean by that.

PROSECUTOR. Neither do I. (*Backs up a few steps.*) Suppose *you* tell me. How close *was* your friendship with the late Mr. Foster's wife?

TRAPP. What are you driving at?

PROSECUTOR. I drive at nothing. I am merely trying to define the exact boundaries of your intimacy with this woman.

TRAPP. "Intimacy"! Who said there was any "intimacy"?

PROSECUTOR. Well, the relationship could hardly have been far from intimate, could it? By your own admission, Mrs. Foster revealed to you the most personal and sensitive secret in her late husband's life. Does a woman reveal such a secret to a man that she knows just casually?

TRAPP. All right, but that doesn't mean—

PROSECUTOR. Mr. Trapp, *when* did Mrs. Foster reveal this secret to you?

TRAPP. When? I don't get you.

PROSECUTOR. What time of day? It wasn't during the morning or the afternoon, was it?

TRAPP. I never said it was—

PROSECUTOR. Of course not. You *worked* during the mornings and afternoons, didn't you? Your contact with Mrs. Foster must have come at *night!*

TRAPP. So what? Her husband's contact with her came at night.

PROSECUTOR. (*Crossing to Trapp.*) Then you admit that your relationship with her was similar to that of a husband?

TRAPP. I didn't admit any such thing—

PROSECUTOR. But surely this wouldn't have been surprising. It would have been the most natural thing in the world. An attractive woman of whom you used to be fond before her marriage—

TRAPP. You're crazy! I never met the woman before her marriage!

PROSECUTOR. Precisely! (*Crossing* R. *to behind his lectern.*) You *weren't* an old childhood friend of hers! You never even met her till after her marriage! Yet your night-time visits to her made her feel so close to you that she was willing to tell you her husband's secrets! Mr. Trapp, what are you afraid of? Why are you ashamed to admit the truth?

TRAPP. (*Confused, annoyed.*) Who's ashamed—

ATTORNEY. (*Rises.*) Your honor, I have kept silent up to now, but I can no longer permit the prosecutor to bully the witness—

TRAPP. Nobody bullies *me!* (*Rises, crosses to* C.) And I've got nothing to be ashamed of, either! (*To Judge.*) It wasn't anything so terrible, for God's sake! I met this Foster woman at a party one night, and she made a play for me! I was feeling pretty rotten just about then. My wife and I weren't getting along— (*To Prosecutor.*) Foster was the boy who got the free trips to Europe in those days, and he was too damned stingy to take his wife with him. So, she was at the party alone; I was at the party alone. All right, I gave in to temptation. Hell, gentlemen, if that's a crime, half the world would be behind bars!

PROSECUTOR. Half the world again. You seem remarkably familiar with the unsavory habits of half the world, Mr. Trapp.

ATTORNEY. I object, your honor. This courtroom is hardly the proper place for the prosecutor to show off his wit.

JUDGE. Objection sustained. Try to restrain yourself, Mr. Prosecutor. (*Attorney sits.*)

PROSECUTOR. I stand corrected. I assure the court it was not my intention to be witty at Mr. Trapp's expense, (*Crossing* C. *to Trapp.*) but rather to express my admiration for his proficiency in dealing with the fair sex. You do have remarkable proficiency, don't you, Mr. Trapp?

TRAPP. (*Preening himself.*) Well, *you* said it. (*Sits.*)

PROSECUTOR. (*Above Trapp's* R. *shoulder.*) And what are your methods, my dear sir? What ingenious gambits do you employ? Would you let us in on some of your little tricks? (*Attorney gestures in objection, Prosecutor and Trapp stop him with waves.*)

TRAPP. No tricks. You have to figure out what a woman really wants out of life, then give it to her. The trouble with most men is, they don't take the time to really *understand* their women.

PROSECUTOR. I see—the techniques of salesmanship applied to the boudoir—

ATTORNEY. (*Rises.*) Your honor, must the dignity of this court be compromised by the prosecutor's taste for smoking-room tittle-tattle?

JUDGE. Mr. Prosecutor, please get on with the questioning. (*Attorney sits.*)

PROSECUTOR. (*Crosses back* R. *behind lectern.*) Of course, your honor. Mr. Trapp—in carrying out your duty of "understanding" the lonely Mrs. Foster, what consideration did you give to the other parties involved? For instance, what were your own wife's feelings in regard to this affair?

TRAPP. I'd be surprised if she had any. She was too busy herself—running around with some crazy poet down in Greenwich Village.

JUDGE. Greenwich Village?

ATTORNEY. A section of New York City, your honor, in which

the Bohemian set usually congregates. A sort of Saint Germain Des Pres in the American style.

JUDGE. Thank you.

PROSECUTOR. In short, Mrs. Trapp's views on understanding are similar to your own?

TRAPP. Mrs. Trapp thinks she has a right to play around as much as she likes—but she sure raises hell when *I* do it. (*Assuming an injured tone.*) Not that I *want* to play around, you understand. She drives me to it. Take tonight. Do you think I'd be going to see this little girl in Geneva tonight if Helen hadn't been making eyes at that ski instructor all week?

PROSECUTOR. (*Crossing* U. L. *to between Trapp and Attorney.*) I see, Mr. Trapp. Your trip to Geneva isn't strictly for business purposes after all. The five thousand dollar commission is actually a delectable young female.

ATTORNEY. (*Rises.*) Your honor, I object. Mr. Trapp's reasons for going to Geneva have nothing whatever to do with the so-called murder.

JUDGE. Objection sustained. (*Attorney sits.*)

TRAPP. (*Rising and crossing* D. R. *to proscenium.*) Yes—I'm getting a little tired of all these personal questions too.

JUDGE. Get back to the murder, Mr. Prosecutor.

PROSECUTOR. As you say, your honor. Mr. Trapp, you've given us an excellent analysis of your extracurricular activities—and your wife's. Now what of the late Mr. Foster? No doubt he was as liberal-minded as Mrs. Trapp?

TRAPP. (*At lectern, fingering book.*) Don't you believe it. The old gang—the old gentleman really cared about his wife.

PROSECUTOR. You mean, he sincerely loved her?

TRAPP. (*Crossing* U. R. *by the bar, looking longingly at the liquor.*) The only thing in the world he *did* love—besides making money and getting his own way.

PROSECUTOR. (*Crossing* D. R. *to edge of proscenium.*) Most interesting. This pompous, stingy, unreasonable tyrant—he really had a soft side to his nature, did he? It was his Achilles' heel, so to speak. (*Trapp crosses to* C.)

TRAPP. How do you mean?

PROSECUTOR. I was merely engaging in idle speculation.

ATTORNEY. Watch out! He *never* engages in idle speculation!

PROSECUTOR. I was merely wondering. Mr. Trapp—in the

course of your affair with Mrs. Foster, did the thought never occur to you that this might be a good way of hurting her husband?

TRAPP. Listen, maybe you've forgotten, but when you sleep with a woman, believe me, you're not thinking about her husband! (*Sits* R. *of table.*)

ATTORNEY. Very true.

PROSECUTOR. (*Assuming a soft, insinuating tone.*) Of course not. Your mind is on more absorbing things. The softness of her flesh, the gentleness of her touch—etcetera etcetera.

TRAPP. (*With a snicker.*) You haven't forgotten so much after all, have you?

PROSECUTOR. (*Crossing to* C.) Unfortunately, no. But what of those other moments in your relationship with the delightful Mrs. Foster? Those delicious moments of rest and peace, when you quietly lay next to her in the bed—what bed, by the way, Mr. Trapp? Yours or hers?

TRAPP. Well, naturally we couldn't use *my* apartment.

PROSECUTOR. Naturally. Her bed then—her bedroom. And as your eyes opened after a night of bliss, how pleasant your feelings must have been towards the objects which greeted your sight. The pattern of the wallpaper, the little bedtable, the dresser just across the room. After all these years you still remember the dear familiar objects on the dresser, (*Joseph usually falls asleep along in here.*) don't you, Mr. Trapp?

TRAPP. (*Grinning at the memory.*) As a matter of fact, I do. She kept a doll there—kind of a toy Pekingese—her good luck pooch, she called it.

PROSECUTOR. And this is the object you remember most vividly?

TRAPP. That, and his grin.

PROSECUTOR. Grin? Whose grin?

TRAPP. Foster's—that picture of him on the dresser, next to the Peke. All dressed up in his evening clothes, grinning away.

PROSECUTOR. Looking very pleased with himself, was he?

TRAPP. You bet he was.

PROSECUTOR. Almost self-satisfied, one might say?

TRAPP. That's exactly what I'd say.

PROSECUTOR. As if he owned the world?

TRAPP. (*Nodding vigorously.*) Yes! (*Laugh.*)

PROSECUTOR. As if he owned his wife?

TRAPP. Yes!

PROSECUTOR. But you knew that he didn't own her, didn't you?

TRAPP. I sure did!

PROSECUTOR. Because you were sharing her with him?

TRAPP. Absolutely!

PROSECUTOR. And that's why you remember that photograph with such pleasure?

TRAPP. Yes.

PROSECUTOR. And that's why you enjoyed sleeping with her in the first place?

TRAPP. Yes— (*Breaks off, confused, shaking his head.*) No, no— that wasn't the main reason—

PROSECUTOR. You admit, then, that it was *one* of the reasons?

ATTORNEY. Your honor, this is most irregular! The Prosecutor is attempting to put words in the defendant's mouth—

PROSECUTOR. (*Crossing* U. C.) It seems to me that I'm drawing them *out* of his mouth! And they finally have the ring of truth!

ATTORNEY. (*Rises.*) Your honor, I object—

PROSECUTOR. All right, all right, I shall gladly discontinue this line of questioning. We've found out all we need to know from it anyway.

TRAPP. (*Still bewildered.*) What've you found out? What—?

PROSECUTOR. Just one thing, Mr. Trapp. We now know, by your own testimony, that your pleasure in having an affair with Mrs. Foster was considerably enhanced by your pleasure in hurting her husband!

TRAPP. But why should I have wanted to hurt him? What was my motive?

PROSECUTOR. We'll come to that in due time perhaps. We agree on one thing, don't we? It would have been a terrible body blow to the late Mr. Foster if he had found out that his wife was carrying on an affair with his own assistant from the office.

TRAPP. (*Gaining confidence, with a laugh.*) *If* he had found out? (*He breaks off, confused again.*)

PROSECUTOR. He *did* find out?

TRAPP. I didn't say that.

PROSECUTOR. But it's the truth, isn't it? What is there in the simple truth that frightens you?

TRAPP. (*Angrily.*) Nothing frightens me!

PROSECUTOR. (*Pounding away.*) Then Mr. Foster *did* find out about the affair?

TRAPP. Even if he did, what difference does it make?

PROSECUTOR. It might make a great deal of difference. You are on trial for murdering this man, and you yourself stated a few moments ago that you had no motive. But suppose the late Foster found out several months or a year before his death that you were carrying on with his wife. What would his reaction be to that? Anger, humiliation, shame—and then the desire for revenge. That's a reasonable assumption, isn't it, Mr. Trapp?

TRAPP. It sounds reasonable.

PROSECUTOR. And how would he proceed to take his revenge? By making use of his superior position in the company, don't you agree? By persecuting you, undermining your confidence, destroying your work, making you look black in the eyes of the top executives. Mr. Foster would use that year to force you out of your job—and you would no doubt go to great lengths to prevent him. There, Mr. Trapp, is your motive for murder!

TRAPP. (*With increased bravado.*) My motive for murder? *That's* my motive for murder? Excuse me, that's funny, that makes me laugh! (*Jumping up and crossing to Prosecutor.*) This whole fancy theory of yours is based on the assumption that Foster found out about his wife and me a year before he died. And the truth is, he found out about us on the day of his death! (*Starts back to his seat, gloating, then realizing he's gone too far.*)

PROSECUTOR. (*Smiling with pleasure.*) The day of his death. Thank you, Mr. Trapp.

JUDGE. Neatly done.

ATTORNEY. (*With a groan.*) Mr. Trapp, are you completely out of your mind?

TRAPP. (*Confused again.*) Why? What's the matter? (*Sits.*)

PROSECUTOR. Mr. Trapp, *how* did Foster find out about the affair?

TRAPP. What do you mean, how?

PROSECUTOR. Did his wife confess the truth to him?

TRAPP. Of course she didn't. She was scared stiff of him.

PROSECUTOR. Did he find it out on his own?

TRAPP. Not him. He was too wrapped up in himself.

PROSECUTOR. Did he stumble on it accidentally then? Did he come home unexpectedly one night?

TRAPP. Oh, come on—I was careful.

PROSECUTOR. (*Crosses* L. C. *to Trapp.*) Then how did Foster find out about the affair?

TRAPP. I don't know, and I damn well don't care!

PROSECUTOR. Mr. Trapp, your reluctance to answer leads me to only one conclusion. *You* told him about the affair.

TRAPP. You're crazy! I never told him!

PROSECUTOR. You did, Mr. Trapp! It's the only possible explanation! I've eliminated all the other possibilities!

TRAPP. (*Jumps up and crosses to* R. *proscenium again.*) You've eliminated Joe Wilson, have you?

PROSECUTOR. Joe Wilson—who was he?

TRAPP. He was one of the other assistants from the office! He was the one who told Foster!

PROSECUTOR. You're asking this court to believe that Joe Wilson told Mr. Foster about the affair?

TRAPP. (*Slamming his fist on the lectern.*) I'm damn well telling this court!

PROSECUTOR. And why did Joe Wilson do that?

TRAPP. He wanted to kill my chances in the company. He always had his eye on my job.

PROSECUTOR. (*Crossing* D. R. *to Trapp.*) But how did the ambitious Joe Wilson find out about the affair in the first place? You certainly didn't tell him.

TRAPP. (*Trapp avoids the Prosecutor by circling around lectern to* C.) Why the hell not?

PROSECUTOR. Because he was your bitterest rival in the company. (*Crossing to behind lectern.*) Because he was bound to go directly to Foster with the information.

TRAPP. Hell, it didn't take him two hours— (*Trapp breaks off, suddenly realizing what he is saying. His swagger is all gone, he looks scared. The Attorney stands up, desperate.*)

ATTORNEY. Your honor, would you instruct the defendant that he need not answer any questions which might tend to incriminate him? (*The Attorney resumes his seat.*)

JUDGE. That's quite true, Mr. Trapp. Your last answer was almost a confession.

TRAPP. (*More frightened. Crosses* U. *to Judge.*) A confession of what? What did I say?

PROSECUTOR. Shall I tell you what you said, Mr. Trapp?

(*Trapp turns.*) You said you were anxious to get ahead in the world by replacing the late Mr. Foster.

TRAPP. (*Coming* D. *a step.*) What's wrong with that? Everybody wants to get ahead!

PROSECUTOR. You said that the late Mr. Foster had a dangerous heart condition. You said that any shock might kill him. You said that you were well aware of this.

TRAPP. (*Crossing to* D. C.) Lots of people were aware of it! His family, his doctor—why aren't *they* on trial?

PROSECUTOR. Because they haven't admitted, as you did, that you deliberately carried on an affair with his wife, (*Crosses* L. *to Trapp.*) and when this affair reached its height you deliberately told your bitterest rival about it—knowing exactly what he would do next. Joe Wilson was your weapon, Mr. Trapp! Through him you struck the fatal blow, just as surely as if your hand had wielded a knife!

TRAPP. (*To Prosecutor.*) No, that's not true! (*Working* D. L.) All right, I was mad at Foster that day—that damned old gangster, he couldn't talk to people as if they were human beings—so the story slipped out while Joe and I were having a couple of beers. (*Working back to* C.) How could I be sure he'd go straight to Foster? How could I be sure that little son-of-a-bitch would have the guts to do a thing like that to *me*?

PROSECUTOR. When the murderer presses the trigger of his gun, Mr. Trapp, how can he be *sure* that the bullet will hit its mark? Your state of assurance is *not* what concerns us! Your *intention* is what concerns us!

TRAPP. (*Crossing* L. *to table.*) What intention? I had no intention!

PROSECUTOR. (*Following him.*) Hadn't you? As you drank your couple of beers and looked across at Joe Wilson, wasn't that the moment when you first said to yourself, "That old gangster Foster is standing in my way! I'd like to kill him!" Wasn't *that* the moment when the idea of murder first entered your head?

TRAPP. No, it wasn't! (*Sits.*)

PROSECUTOR. The moment was earlier then? When, Mr. Trapp? Was it the moment you opened your eyes and saw Mr. Foster's picture grinning at you from his wife's dresser?

TRAPP. No—I never thought such a thing—

PROSECUTOR. Earlier still, in other words? Yes, of course—it was the moment you first heard about Foster's heart condition! *That* was when you got the idea, wasn't it?

TRAPP. No, no—

PROSECUTOR. In that case, it must have been way back at the very beginning—when you first started your affair with Mrs. Foster! That's how it was, wasn't it, Mr. Trapp? The idea to murder Foster came into your head at the same moment as the idea to sleep with his wife!

TRAPP. Why do you keep talking about that damned affair? As if it was something important in my life!

PROSECUTOR. I'm mistaken in that assumption?

TRAPP. Damn right you're mistaken. I cut that thing off fast enough!

PROSECUTOR. You did?

TRAPP. I did! I told her I was through with her—

PROSECUTOR. When?

TRAPP. (*Triumphantly.*) The day after Foster's funeral—I told her— (*Realizes he's said too much again.*)

PROSECUTOR. (*Smiling grimly. Quietly, drawing Trapp out.*) The day after Foster's funeral. When your use for the unfortunate Mrs. Foster was over—when the affair had served its purpose.

TRAPP. There wasn't any purpose!

PROSECUTOR. Wasn't there, Mr. Trapp? Think back! Even as you smiled at that woman for the first time, at that moment, wasn't there something inside of you—a voice, a feeling, an impulse—something saying "I can use this for my own purposes—I don't know when, I don't know how, but I can use this to get rid of her husband." Wasn't that the moment the idea first came into your head?

TRAPP. No, I wouldn't listen to it!

PROSECUTOR. Listen to what?

TRAPP. I pushed it out of my mind!

PROSECUTOR. The impulse that told you to murder Foster?

TRAPP. I swear to God, I kept pushing it out of my mind, pushing it out of my mind!

PROSECUTOR. (*Pause.*) Your honor, the prosecution rests its case. (*Long silence, while Trapp, stunned, bewildered, frightened, stares straight ahead. The Prosecutor resumes his seat.*)

JUDGE. Has the defense attorney any questions to ask the witness?

ATTORNEY. No, your honor—no questions.

JUDGE. The Defense will now present its case.

ATTORNEY. Your Honor, under the circumstances my case will have to be contained in my summation.

JUDGE. Very well then. Court will be recessed, so that you gentlemen may prepare your summations. (*Strikes his gavel. The Judge starts across the foyer to the stairs, the Attorney and Prosecutor start* U.)

TRAPP. (*A gleam of hope.*) It's all over? The trial is over?

JUDGE. (*At middle of foyer.*) Oh no. We are merely retiring temporarily. We'll be back.

PROSECUTOR. (*Half-way up bottom steps, turns around.*) That's a promise, Mr. Trapp. (*Left alone, Trapp stares around the room. Sees the exit is blocked by the dozing Old Man. He thinks a moment, then tiptoes to kitchen door and calls out in a loud whisper.*)

TRAPP. Nicole! (*Nicole comes in from the kitchen. She has her hat, coat, and boots on.*)

NICOLE. It's about time. I was just going to leave.

TRAPP. (*Taking her arm, gesturing to Old Man.*) Come here. I don't want him to hear us.

NICOLE. (*Crossing* U. C.) Oh, he is a very sound sleeper. Nothing can wake him. (*Crosses* D. C.) Well, Monsieur, are we now about to have that conversation?

TRAPP. (*Crossing* D. *to her, trying to sound casual.*) I've got a better idea. As long as you're all ready, maybe I could drive down to the village with you. We could go dancing.

NICOLE. But Monsieur Carpeau expects you to spend the night.

TRAPP. But I'd rather be with you.

NICOLE. (*Crossing* D. R.) The driving will not be easy in this storm.

TRAPP. (*Following her.*) I like to live dangerously.

NICOLE. (*Ponders a moment, then shakes her head, moving* U. R.) No, Monsieur Carpeau will be offended.

TRAPP. (*Crossing to her.*) I fixed it with him—I got his permission.

NICOLE. Then you have finished playing the game?

TRAPP. Yes, the game's over. They all went up to bed.

NICOLE. (*Crossing to foot of steps, gesturing.*) But the old gentleman, Monsieur Pillet, *he* hasn't gone to bed.

TRAPP. (*Following her.*) He was asleep—they didn't want to

wake him. Come on, let's get going. (*Offering his hand, they start toward the kitchen.*)

NICOLE. (*Smiling, moving with him.*) Very well. (*Suddenly turning back and crossing* R.) I'll just go up and say good night to Monsieur Carpeau.

TRAPP. (*Uncontrollably raising his voice and grabbing her.*) No.

NICOLE. Monsieur? Why are you so excited?

TRAPP. (*Crossing* L. *to behind witness chair.*) They're going to . . . I don't know what they're going to do to me if you don't get me out of here!

NICOLE. (*Crossing* D. C.) But why should they do anything to you?

TRAPP. They're crazy! All four of them!

NICOLE. Crazy? They are fine, intelligent men.

TRAPP. (*Desperate, bends and grasps* L. *table with both hands for support.*) This game of theirs . . . the people who play it with them . . . my God, they could sentence you to hang!

NICOLE. (*With a smile.*) Oh no, Monsieur. Only if they find you guilty.

TRAPP. (*Stunned, slowly straightening up in horror.*) You *know?* . . .

NICOLE. (*Crossing* D. C.) The rules of the game are most familiar to me. If they find you innocent, there can be no hanging. And they *have* found you innocent, haven't they? Otherwise Monsieur Carpeau would not have given you permission to drive into the village tonight. (*Crossing* L. *to level with him, sweetly.*) Or were you lying to me, Monsieur?

TRAPP. (*Desperate, backing a step.*) No—they *did* find me innocent. . . .

NICOLE. (*A beat, then.*) You *are* lying, Monsieur. (*Crossing back* U. C.) It it natural, of course. A condemned man will do many things, out of desperation. But I am so sorry, I cannot take you down the mountain. (*Crossing to bottom of steps.*) Monsieur Carpeau and his friends would be disappointed. . . . It would be ungrateful of me.

TRAPP. (*Following* U. C.) Ungrateful? I don't understand.

NICOLE. After everything they have done for me? It was they who paid all my medical expenses during my years in the hospital.

TRAPP. I don't understand.

NICOLE. (*Crossing* D. C.) After I had my breakdown . . . who else was there to help me? Poor Pierre was in prison.

TRAPP. Pierre . . . ?

NICOLE. But didn't you know, Monsieur, that I am Pierre's sister? A terrible thing was done to me when I was very young, and Pierre killed the man who did it . . . and then I had my breakdown. But now I am well again, thanks to Monsieur Carpeau and his friends.

TRAPP. (*Horrified, realizing his hopeless position.*) You're as crazy as they are, you're in on the whole . . .

NICOLE. (*Taking her keys out of her pocket and starting up the steps.*) Good night, Monsieur. If I don't see you in the morning, it has been a pleasure . . . (*She starts to the front door, Trapp makes a lunge for the keys.*)

TRAPP. God damn you, give me those keys to your car! (*But before he can get them away from her, Pierre comes in menacingly, Trapp staggers back in fear.*)

NICOLE. It's all right, Pierre, Mr. Trapp was only saying good night. (*She smiles at him, turns, and leaves the house. Trapp, all the spirit gone out of him, sinks into* U. R. *chair. Pierre mounts the platform and takes up his position as the Judge, Attorney and Prosecutor, come down the stairs and take up their places.*)

JUDGE. Well, here we are, Mr. Trapp . . . just as I promised. (*Raps his gavel.*) Court is once more in session. (*Pierre comes* D. *and leads Trapp back to the witness stand, and returns to his position.*) Gentlemen, are you ready with your summations?

PROSECUTOR. Ready, Your Honor.

ATTORNEY. Ready, Your Honor.

JUDGE. You may begin.

ATTORNEY. (*Rising.*) Thank you, Your Honor. (*He pats Trapp's shoulder. As his speech goes on, Trapp slowly emerges from his lethargy, listens more and more closely.*) Courage, my friend, I have performed miracles before. (*Crossing* U. C.) Your Honor, gentlemen, this case has presented peculiar difficulties for me as you know. I am accustomed to conducting my cases in my own way, facing no obstacles other than the carefully laid traps of my respected opponent. I am *not* accustomed to finding my greatest enemy right in my own camp. And yet—here is the significant point—this very obstacle turns out to be the basis of my defense. Gentlemen, you observed the heedlessness with which my client plunged into this trial, his artless frankness in bringing out facts which were damaging to his own case. Was this the attitude of a guilty man? Could any man with murder on his conscience conceivably conduct himself in this manner? No, gentlemen, he could not. Mr. Trapp protested his innocence because he *is* innocent—in his mind.

Mark those three simple words—in his mind. The facts may be against him. Indeed it would be futile for me to deny it. He did hate his chief and covet his job—what employee doesn't? He did make love to his chief's wife, confess the affair to his bitter rival and ultimately cause the late lamented Foster's death by heart failure—but *in his mind* he committed no murder. He started off with no grand plan which he then cunningly and cold-bloodedly set into motion. He proceeded rather by fits and starts. In this connection, gentlemen, let us not forget that voice, feeling, impulse which the prosecutor so cleverly brought into the testimony—that impulse of guilt or greed or suppressed desire, or what you will. This impulse, if you recall, persistently insinuated itself into Mr. Trapp's mind and suggested to him that he wanted to kill the late Foster—and just as persistently, Mr. Trapp rejected the suggestion, recoiled from the impulse in horror. There, in a nutshell, is the pattern of all his actions—recoiling in his conscious mind from the very thing towards which his subconscious mind is pushing him.

In this respect, gentlemen, the defendant is not much different from the rest of mankind—that is, he is *unconscious* of the implications of what he does. His behavior is mean—granted. Selfish—granted. Ignoble—granted. But human, gentlemen, overwhelmingly, devastatingly human—and therefore worthy of our pity, our compassion, our forgiveness. For what is life, after all, but a chaotic battlefield in which we all more or less contribute every day to the murder of our fellow citizens—while they are just as industriously murdering us. Our good friend, our dear friend, Howard Trapp is not responsible for this sad state of affairs—and we have no right to punish him for it. Thank you. (*The Attorney returns to his chair. Sits.*)

TRAPP. (*Nodding, feeling more confident.*) That's right—I just live the way everybody else does. You can't blame me for that.

JUDGE. Mr. Prosecutor, your summation, if you please.

PROSECUTOR. Thank you, Your Honor. (*He rises. Trapp listens intently, his confidence receding, his fear growing as the Prosecutor talks. Crossing* U. C.) Your Honor, Gentlemen, I have listened with the greatest interest to the words of my distinguished colleague, and it will perhaps surprise you to hear that I agree with almost everything he said. Gentlemen, the defense comes right out and admits the essential fact—that murder was done. It merely seeks to justify this by the extraordinary statement that the defendant is like the rest of mankind, that he moves along unconsciously from passion to passion, from selfishness to selfishness.

Gentlemen, who denies this? Of all people in the world, certainly not we! What on earth is the whole point of this court, its whole reason for being, if not to deal with so-called "unconscious" criminals like Mr. Trapp? Gentlemen, the sacred duty of this court is to unearth, condemn, and punish without hesitation those crimes which the formally-constituted agencies of the law are unable to reach. Have we ever allowed the plea of "unconsciousness" to sway us from this duty? We recognize the true nature of Mr. Trapp's unconsciousness, that voice, that feeling, that impulse which in his own words he kept pushing out of his mind. He rejected it in horror but he killed the late Mr. Foster anyway. Thus his very rejection of the impulse became his most powerful rationalization. "How could I have meant to commit murder when I recoiled so violently from the idea of committing murder?" This is your unconsciousness, gentlemen! "Unconsciousness"—that most insidious of narcotics in our addled modern world, that quick complacent justification for all our sins. Naturally such a criminal as Mr. Trapp is unconscious of his actions. Naturally he feels no pangs of guilt. What is this but another way of saying that he is too thick-skinned even to have a conscience?

My distinguished colleague says that the whole world is like this, that life is a battlefield occupied by unthinking, unfeeling savages. I refuse to believe this. Men do not *all* behave like brutes—but the brute is *in* us all—fighting to take control of us. And when we give in to it, we justify our weakness by saying "Everybody acts the same way, it's not me . . . it's my unconscious mind." The purpose of this court is to fight this brute who lies hidden inside every man . . . to help in our small way to stamp it out—

by stamping out those individuals who have allowed it to turn them into destroyers of their fellow men. Howard Trapp is just such a destructive force, and the prosecution demands that he pay for his crime with his life! (*The Prosecutor resumes his seat.*)

TRAPP. (*Breaking in, horrified.*) You really mean it, don't you?

JUDGE. Well, it looks as if my moment has come—

TRAPP. You'd really like to see me dead, wouldn't you?

JUDGE. (*Hits gavel.*) Mr. Trapp—

TRAPP. (*Wildly, jumping to his feet. Crossing* U. C.) No, I have something to say. I'm sick and tired of your game! I'm quitting! (*Pierre jumps up.*) Trial's over!

PROSECUTOR. (*Rising.*) Mr. Trapp, you pledged yourself to follow it through to the end.

ATTORNEY. (*Rising.*) That's quite true, Mr. Trapp.

JUDGE. We haven't released you from your pledge.

TRAPP. I release myself! I just won't sit in on your trial any more.

ATTORNEY. You really ought to be present while your fate is being decided.

TRAPP. My fate! What have you lunatics got to do with my fate? My fate is in my own hands!

JUDGE. Not so, Mr. Trapp. When a man appears before the law, he temporarily places his fate in the hands of others.

TRAPP. You're not the law! You're not a goddamn thing! This court is just a figment of your imaginations—this court doesn't even exist!

JUDGE. It exists in this house.

TRAPP. All right, I'll leave this house. (*He rushes to door* R., *runs up against Pierre, who takes his arm firmly. Trapp's bravado collapses, and he is crushed, frightened.*)

JUDGE. Pierre—will you please escort Mr. Trapp to the bench? (*Pierre leads him* D. *to in front of Judge.*) I hate to put you to the inconvenience—but I'm afraid that's the way it's always done.— Mr. Trapp, it is now my duty to pass sentence on you. A grave duty—often an unpleasant duty—and yet, not entirely without its compensations. For I'm sure you will agree with me that the feelings and fate of any one individual are of relatively minor importance compared to the grand, the awesome questions which hang in the balance tonight. Whatever may happen to you, one good thing will come out of this trial. The ends of justice will be served. Mr. Trapp, I sincerely believe your plea of unconsciousness. I understand it, I sympathize with it, but unfortunately I find no legal significance in it. Your crime has been proven, and only one course remains to me. I hereby sentence you to death by hanging. And may God have mercy on your soul. (*Trapp, in shock, slowly sits. A long silence, then the Prosecutor and Attorney get up, laugh, and Attorney crosses to Prosecutor.*)

ATTORNEY. Well, you old scoundrel! You did it again, didn't you?

PROSECUTOR. Yes, you old rascal! (*The Judge goes to the bar and pours three brandies.*)

ATTORNEY. (*Pierre leads Trapp to witness chair, then goes to bar to help with drinks.*) Your tactics were completely unscrupulous, of course—but brilliant, I have to admit it. Congratulations, you deserve your victory.

PROSECUTOR. If you hadn't been hampered by certain circumstances beyond your control, I feel sure *I* would be congratulating you.

JUDGE. (*Coming* U. *with drinks.*) His line of questioning was magnificent. Of course, you could never have gotten away with it in any other court.

ATTORNEY. Let's drink on it to show there are no hard feelings.

PROSECUTOR. No hard feelings.

JOSEPH. (*Suddenly appears in doorway* R.) Will you be needing me tonight?

JUDGE. Good Heavens, we forgot Joseph!

ATTORNEY. Poor Joseph!

PROSECUTOR. An unfortunate oversight.

JUDGE. A new triumph for the prosecution, Joseph. Another death sentence.

JOSEPH. Congratulations, Gustave. (*Goes up to Prosecutor, shakes his hand.*)

PROSECUTOR. Thank you, Joseph. (*Pierre goes to top of steps, stands.*)

JUDGE. Well now—it's late, and we're all quite tired. Joseph, will you escort Mr. Trapp upstairs? (*For the first time they all turn and look at Trapp.*)

TRAPP. (*Slowly growing frightened again.*) Upstairs—?

JOSEPH. If you please, Mr. Trapp. (*He goes up to Trapp, gently holds out his hand.*)

TRAPP. (*With a shudder.*) I don't want to go upstairs. (*Joseph crosses* L. *to Attorney.*)

ATTORNEY. Mr. Trapp, what's wrong? The trial is over. You must go upstairs.

JUDGE. (*Gesturing.*) Pierre—help Mr. Trapp. (*Pierre approaches Trapp. Trapp, in a panic, turns* U.)

TRAPP. No! (*He faces them all, his control going.*) All right—all right, maybe I did it! Maybe I did want him dead, and made sure of it. When I was a kid I found out it's dog-eat-dog in this world, so why shouldn't I be better at it than anyone else! You're murderers, too—murderers just as much as I am! Only you call it justice! What's justice? I don't believe in justice! There's no such thing as justice! There's no such thing as justice! (*Before they can move he rushes* U. *to the foyer, spins around to face them, starts backing around the corner post and up onto the Judge's platform. They start closing in on him, as he reaches for the latch on the backing windows. The lights fade slowly.*)

ACT II

Scene 2

It is several evenings later. The room is arranged as it was at the beginning of the play. The Prosecutor and Attorney are playing chess in the C. *of the room. The Judge stands over them, watching the game. The Old Man is in his easy chair* L., *placidly smoking his pipe. The front doorbell rings. The Judge looks up curiously, while Nicole enters from the kitchen* L. *and crosses the foyer. She opens the front door* R. *to Helen Trapp, who wears a touch of mourning but looks very chic. We see that it is a pleasant evening outside, no sign of a storm.*

HELEN. Excuse me—could I see Mr. Emile Carpeau? (*Nicole nods. The Judge sees Helen and goes out to the hall to meet her. Nicole returns to the kitchen* L.)

JUDGE. Yes—can I help you?

HELEN. Mr. Carpeau, I'm Helen Trapp.

JUDGE. Oh, yes—the unfortunate gentleman's wife.

HELEN. I don't want to disturb you—but I'm flying back to America tomorrow—and thought, before I left—

JUDGE. You wished to talk with someone who was near your husband at the end. Very natural, Mrs. Trapp. Won't you come in and meet my friends?

HELEN. Thank you. (*The Judge leads her into the living room. The others stand up as she enters.*)

JUDGE. Gentlemen, this is Mrs. Trapp—the wife of poor Mr. Trapp. (*He indicates each one in turn, and each man gives a murmur of sympathy and acknowledgement.*) Mr. Bernard Laroque—Mr. Gustave Kummer—Mr. Joseph Pillet. Now won't you sit down? (*She sits in* R. *chair. Prosecutor sits back at* L. *of chess table.*)

HELEN. Thank you. I just came because—well, Howard and I had an argument before he left the other day, and I just wanted to be sure—

JUDGE. That this argument had no connection with the tragedy? Yes, I see what agony of mind you must be in. Well, let me reassure you—your husband's death was an accident . . . he drank a bit too much, grew somewhat confused, and rushed out into the storm. In the dark, he couldn't possibly have seen the precipice before he fell over it.

PROSECUTOR. He must have died instantly—his neck was broken, you know.

ATTORNEY. (*Crossing to above her chair.*) In any event, you have no reason to reproach yourself.

HELEN. (*Relieved.*) Thank heaven!

PROSECUTOR. (*Fixing her with his sharp, appraising look. Rising and crossing* R. *to in front of* R. *chess chair.*) It's sad, at your age, to lose a husband to whom you were no doubt deeply devoted.

HELEN. (*Almost peremptorily.*) Oh yes, very sad.

PROSECUTOR. You know, your husband spoke of you at dinner that night.

HELEN. (*Uneasily.*) I can't imagine what he said about me.

JUDGE. (*Exchanging a significant look with Prosecutor.*) Nothing which at all displeased us, believe me. In fact, he made you seem quite—appealing to us.

ATTORNEY. (*Also catching the Prosecutor's significant look.*) We were terribly interested to know you—after what he said.

PROSECUTOR. Oh yes, he spoke quite feelingly of your life together.

HELEN. (*A little puzzled.*) —He did?

JUDGE. Mrs. Trapp, it'll be dark in a few minutes, and the ride down the mountain takes several hours. Why don't you stay and have dinner with us?

HELEN. Oh no, I couldn't put you to the inconvenience.

JUDGE. It won't be any inconvenience, I assure you.

PROSECUTOR. There's always more than enough food.

ATTORNEY. We'll be very disappointed if you say no. (*The Old Man steps forward, smiles gently, and speaks in a quavering but persuasive voice.*)

OLD MAN. For my sake, Madame—to please an old man?

HELEN. Well, I *am* rather worn out just now— (*She hesitates a moment longer, then smiles.*) All right, I'd love to stay. (*The four men nod and cry out with delight at this.*)

JUDGE. Let me give you some cognac—a very special brand.

ATTORNEY. (*Helping her off with her coat.*) You know, it's been so long since we entertained a lady in this house, it will really be quite a novelty. (*He gives a smile of special pleasure. He goes* U. *to coatrack with coat, then comes* D. *again.*)

JUDGE. And after dinner, perhaps we can think of something amusing to do—just to take your mind off your troubles. Perhaps some little parlor game . . . (*The four men laugh gaily, and Helen, quite charmed and flattered, joins in. The curtain slowly falls.*)

END OF THE PLAY

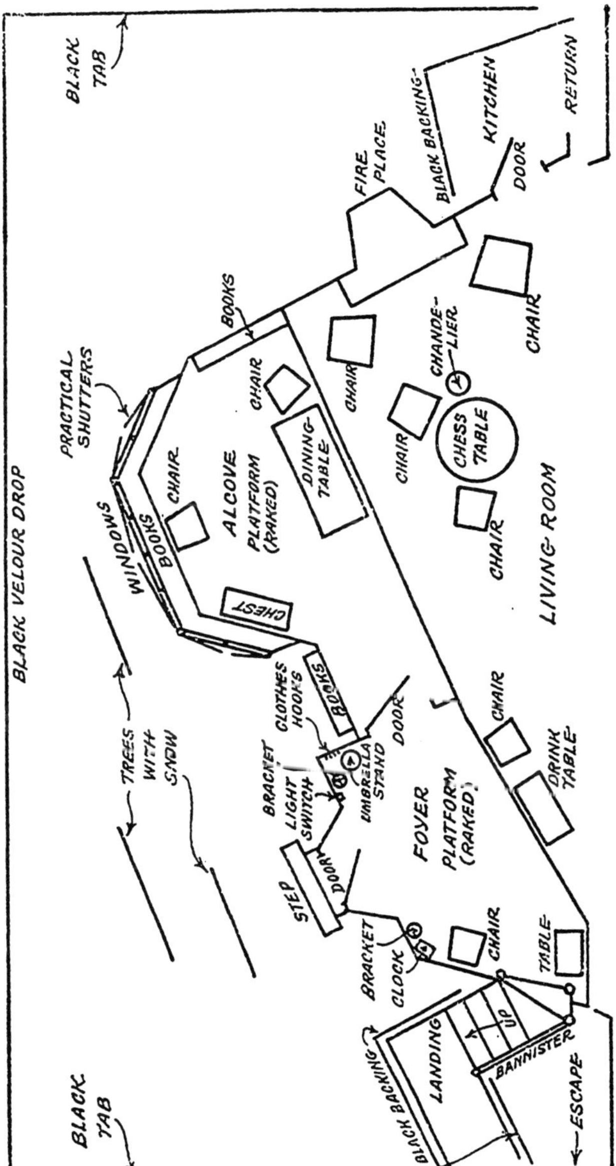

SCENE DESIGN
"THE DEADLY GAME"

PROPERTY PLOT

FURNITURE:

Foyer:
- Table
- Chair
- Antler coat rack
- Umbrella stand

Living Room:
- Drink table
- Chess table with drawer upstage
- 2 small armchairs at chess table
- 2 armchairs by fireplace
- Sidechair by drink table

Alcove:
- Dining table with drawer upstage
- Chair left of table
- Chair under center window
- Chest for blanket (and wardrobe during quick change under right window)

DRESSING: stage right to stage left
- On stair backing: 2 pictures
- On foyer table: Ivy in vase
- On wall right of exterior door: Clock
- In umbrella stand: Umbrellas and canes
- On wall left of exterior door: Antlers and clothes hooks
- On clothes hooks: Overcoats
- On window sills:
  - 2 pots with flowers under right window
  - 2 pots with flowers under right center window
  - 3 pots with flowers under left window
- On windows:
  - Lace curtains and draperies on rods with tiebacks
- On bookcase upper left:
  - 4 pewter mugs
  - Diploma
  - Pewter pitcher
- In all bookcases: Books and magazines

On wall upstage of mantel: 2 pictures
On wall over mantel:
  Plate
  3 sets of antlers
On mantel:
  Candlestick
  2 vases
  Framed photograph
In Fireplace: Andiron, wood, tools
On wall down stage of mantel: 2 pictures, diploma
On wall over down left door: Large portrait
On armchairs: Antimacassars
In alcove and living room: Carpets
Offstage: Snow covered trees

ACT I

Chimes right, 7 strikes
Bell in foyer (practical, operated from offstage)
Lantern on floor by umbrella stand
Drapes in alcove open

On dining table
  Cloth
  4 plates
  4 knives
  4 forks
  2 serving spoons
  Carving fork and knife

In dining table drawer
  Fork
  Knife
  Plate
  5 napkins
  Pad, pencil and gavel (for JUDGE in Act II)
On chair by drink table: Blanket

On drink table
  Ashtray and matches
  4 wine glasses
  Sherry glass
  Sherry decanter
  Corkscrew
  Brandy decanter
  2 snifters

On chess table

Ashtray

Chessgame set up (DEF. ATT. RIGHT, WHITE JUDGE LEFT BLACK)

Off right:

Snow, water and glycerine to wet down actors

Snow cradles over door and window filled

Fans to blow snow

Off left:

Bottle of Medoc

Bottle of Chambertin with loose cork

Tray with 4 sherry glasses

Salt and pepper shakers

Platter on which is:

- Goose
- Goose slices (bananas)
- Mushrooms on buns
- Asparagus
- Gravy boat and spoon with gravy

Coffee tray on which is:

- 5 demi-tasse cups
- 5 saucers
- coffee in cups

Tea trolley on which is:

- Souffle in casserole
- Chafing dish
- 5 plates
- 2 serving spoons
- 5 spoons

DOORS CLOSED, DRAPES OPEN

PERSONAL:

JUDGE:

3 cigars

Wooden matches

Glasses

TRAPP:

Photo in case

Cigarettes

PROSECUTOR:

Cigarettes

Cigarette case
Monocle
Cigarette lighter

DEFENSE ATTORNEY:
Pince nez
Cigarette lighter
Bonbonniere with candy

NICHOLE:
Car keys

PIERRE:
Kitchen matches

ELECTRIC:
2 brackets in foyer
Fire effect in fireplace
Candle on mantel
2 chandeliers, alcove and living room
Wall switch for brackets left of exterior door

WARDROBE:

JUDGE: Tuxedo, congress gaiters, watch and chain, legal robe and hat.

DEFENSE ATTORNEY: Tails, gaiters, silk scarf, legal robe and hat.

PIERRE: Tuxedo, gaiters, wrist warmers, scarf, watch and chain.

TRAPP: Suit, overcoat, overshoes, gloves, hat, scarf, trousers for change.

PROSECUTOR: Overcoat, hat, gloves, tuxedo, overshoes, scarf, pumps, legal robe and hat.

HELEN: Black dress, fur coat, handbag.

OLD MAN: Pipe.

ACT II—*Scene* 1

Clear dining table
Clear glasses from mantel
Clear drink table except ashtray
Clear chess table
Set chair above dining table with cushion for Judge
Set drink table and chair in Act II marks

Set brandy and 4 glasses on mantel, upstage corner
Set one dining table chair under left window
Set one chess table chair under left bookcase
Strike Trapp's scarf
Check chess table and down left armchair in Act II marks
Sweep foyer

Off left:
Briefcase, 2 books, pencil, notepaper, DEFENSE ATTORNEY
Gavel, pencil, paper, JUDGE
Notebook, pencil, PROSECUTOR
Pre-set chessboard for II—2 change
DOORS CLOSED

ACT II—*Scene 2*

Set (on Act I marks):
Drink table
Drink table chair
Chess table
Chess table chairs
Armchairs
Set brandy and glasses on dining table
Set pre-set chess board on chess table

Strike:
Books
Pencils
Briefcase
Gavel
Legal hats
Trapp's coat and hat and overshoes
Actors put robes out of window, take coats from chest under right window
DOORS CLOSED